ReAwakening

THE POWER OF THE GOSPEL

Dr. Bobby M. Wagner

Bladensburg, MD

ReAwakening
The Power of the Gospel

Published by
Dove Christian Publishers
P.O. Box 611
Bladensburg, MD 20710-0611
www.dovechristianpublishers.com

Copyright © 2020 by Bobby Wagner

Cover Design by Faith Darden

ISBN: 9781734303247

Library of Congress Control No.: 2020902511

All rights reserved. No part of this publication may be used or reproduced without permission of the publisher, except for brief quotes for scholarly use, reviews or articles.

All Scripture quotations in this book, except those noted otherwise, are from the NEW AMERICAN STANDARD BIBLE®, Copyright © 1960,1962,1963,1968,1971,1972,1973,1975,1977,1995 by The Lockman Foundation. Used by permission.

Scripture quoted by permission. Quotations designated (NET) are from the NET Bible® copyright ©1996, 2019 by Biblical Studies Press, L.L.C. http://netbible.com

Quotations marked ESV are taken from The ESV® Bible (The Holy Bible, English Standard Version®) copyright © 2001 by Crossway, a publishing ministry of Good News Publishers.

Quotations marked NIV are taken from THE HOLY BIBLE, NEW INTERNATIONAL VERSION®, NIV® Copyright © 1973, 1978, 1984, 2011 by Biblical, Inc. ® Used by permission. All rights reserved worldwide.

Printed in the United States of America

Acknowledgments

I want to thank my God for the incredible privilege of sharing in His mission to the world. Thank You, Father, for calling me and revealing Your incredible plan and wisdom to a sinful man like me. Your ways are so far above our ways. Each and every day, I become more overwhelmed with Your plan, that You would love us so much that You would send Your one and only Son to reveal Yourself to those who believe, that through the Gospel of Jesus Christ, the church becomes one with You and shares in Your glory. Words can never express my gratitude.

Thank You, Jesus, for manifesting the love of God to me personally. Thank You for the perfect life You live for me; thank You for Your death on the cross that has forgiven me all my sins, and thank You for Your resurrection that has changed and transformed my life forever. Thank You for the incredible example You have given me to follow in life, death, and resurrection. Thank You, Holy Spirit, for Your incredible resurrection power that has raised me to new life. I am so amazed that You have given me all the power I need to fulfill the mission that the Savior has given me. Thank You that You love me just as the Father and the Son do. I stand in awe that You have filled me with the mind of Christ.

I want to also thank my family for their incredible support during the process. I want to first thank my wife, Melina, who has been an inspiration to me through this journey. She has taken care of four children (including myself) during this process and has never complained about my absence. Without my wife, this process would have been impossible. She and I have learned what living out the Gospel is all about, and this book is just as much hers as it is mine. I would also like to thank my girls, Trinity, Eden, and Faith, who inspire me every day and were extremely patient with Daddy during completion of the book. I would like to also thank my mom Lisa, who helped out wherever she could. Thank You, Mom, for always being there for us.

Thank You, Pastor Scott Wager. You have been a close friend, colleague, and example during this entire process. Finally, I would like to thank my church family at ReAwakening Church that supported me during the process.

Table of Contents

Acknowledgments iii

Your Eternal Identity 1

The Greatest Identity 9

Why We Need a ReAwakening 20

Why Are We Here? 36

The Foundation 47

What is the Good News? 56

A Closer Look 67

The Complete Gospel 82

What Now? 106

Notes 126

Bibliography 127

Your Eternal Identity

Have you ever wanted your life to count for something? If you had only one day left to live, what would you do? Everyone is motivated by something. Life is a precious gift, but if you were standing at death's door right now, would you be able to define why you lived your life the way you did? Was it because of family? Money? Fame? Take as much time as you need to answer that question, because what motivates your life determines your destiny.

How will your children remember you? How will anyone remember you? Will anyone remember you at all? What will your epitaph read? Ponder those questions for a moment and write down how you want the world to remember you. You can even go a step further and write what you would want people to hear in your obituary. The legacy you leave will impact your eternity.

The biggest factor in determining your legacy can be found in your identity, that which shapes your life, behavior, and character. I write extensively about this in my second book, *Identity Cri-*

sis. I highly recommend that book for more in-depth study. Unfortunately, most of us find our identity in our hurts, fears, and failures. Or, maybe we find our identity in bad parents, bad teachers, or bad examples. Sometimes, the worst crisis in our lives makes us create protective walls around our lives so we don't get hurt again. This is not our true identity. Crisis takes our power away. It is our kryptonite.

The greatest fear in our world today is death, and the fear of death renders us powerless. Many of us live with a great fear of death, but death helps us understand where our power lies. There are two kinds of death: physical and spiritual. We see physical death every day, not only on television programs filled with violence but also in our daily lives as the result of murder, sickness, and accidents. That is the death we fear, and it is only a temporal death. Spiritual death, on the other hand, is what we experience when we refuse to submit to the God of all creation due to our rebellious, sinful nature, which causes us to turn to the temporal things and away from the eternal things that give us the power we were created for. Spiritual death is eternal. If the world's greatest fear is temporal death, how much more should we fear eternal, spiritual death?

There is Good News (Gospel) of great joy for all the people. Death loses its power over our lives when we believe the Gospel and ReAwaken our power-filled identity. Eventually, every person will realize the world of sin we live in will never be able to provide eternal life, the true identity that God has written on the hearts of all people (Eccl. 3:11). At that point, we will turn from the temporal world of sin that guarantees death and ReAwaken to the God who promises eternal life (Eph. 2:1-2). The bottom line is that we all have only one life to live, and when we ReAwaken to the life God created us for, we find power.

Turning from the natural life that we all have experienced and ReAwakening to the eternal life that God provides is the only way we can experience a life characterized by power, fulfillment, contentment, purpose, and meaning that extends beyond the grave. Living for this temporal life will only produce an identity characterized by a powerless life, as well as a lack of purpose and meaning. In other words, "You will never ReAwaken unless you find something worth dying for." Living for the eternal life that God provides will give you something worth dying for and living powerfully for.

Many of us may find dying for something a difficult concept to digest. But soldiers give their lives to protect their countries every day. Servants of worldly leaders are willing to die for their kings. In his book *True Discipleship*, Christian missionary and preacher William MacDonald records a letter written by an American college student who had been converted to Communism in Mexico that demonstrates how loyal Communists are to their cause. The letter was read by Billy Graham:

> *We Communists have a high casualty rate. We're the ones who get shot and hung and lynched and tarred and feathered and jailed and slandered and ridiculed and fired from our jobs, and in every other way made as uncomfortable as possible. A certain percentage of us get killed or imprisoned.*

We live in virtual poverty. We turn back to the party every penny we make above what is absolutely necessary to keep us alive. We Communists don't have the time or the money for many movies, or concerts, or T-bone steaks, or decent homes and new cars. We've been described as fanatics. We are fanatics. Our lives are dominated by one great overshadowing factor, THE STRUGGLE FOR WORLD COMMUNISM. We Communists have a philosophy of life which no amount of money could buy. We have a cause to fight for, a definite purpose in life. We subordinate our petty, personal selves into a great movement of humanity, and if our personal lives seem hard, or our egos appear to suffer through subordination to the party, then we are adequately compensated by the thought that each of us in his small way is contributing to something new and true and better for mankind. There is one thing in which I am in dead earnest and that is the Communist cause. It is my life, my business, my religion, my hobby, my sweetheart, my wife and mistress, my bread and meat. I work at it in the daytime and dream of it at night. Its hold on me grows, not lessens as time goes on. Therefore, I cannot carry on a friendship, a love affair, or even a conversation without relating it to this force which both drives and guides my life. I evaluate people, books, ideas, and actions according to how they affect the Communist cause and by their attitude toward it. I've already been in jail because of my ideas and if necessary, I'm ready to go before a firing squad.[1]

If Communists give their lives for Communism, how much more should Christians pour themselves out in complete obedience to their Lord and King? McDonald said, "Surely if the Lord Jesus is worth anything, He is worth everything." [2] If we as human beings are willing and able to die for something temporary, how much more should we be willing to die for something eternal?

Many of us live our lives with an incredible emptiness because we never fill that God-shaped hole in our hearts with the one thing that is worth dying for. It is a gruesome feeling, always trying to fill our God-shaped hole with sex, drugs, rock n roll, the perfect job, the perfect spouse, lots of money, and whatever we think will make us happy. When none of these things fill that God-shaped hole in our hearts, we begin sensing something is missing. A powerless life. As a result, we begin asking ourselves a very important question: "What is my purpose in this life?" We begin feeling an overwhelming sense of gloom as we try to figure it out. We continue to spin our wheels through a life of crisis, going through the same old routine day in and day out with no real power. In the meantime, that God-shaped hole is always intrinsically sensing that something is missing. I am reminded of an old song, "There is a God-shaped hole in all of us that can only be filled by You." If we don't fill our God-shaped hole with the correct identity, we will never ReAwaken to that one thing that is worth dying for.

ReAwakening your power-filled identity cannot be found in the physical world but in the spiritual world that Jesus Christ has enabled us to enter through His life, death on the cross, and resurrection. When we ReAwaken to the spiritual kingdom, we bring the manifestation of God's kingdom power to the physical realm.

It is the only way we can impact lives and leave a lasting legacy. It is the only way we will ReAwaken our power-filled identity and discover rest for our souls. As Saint Augustine once said, "You stir man in taking pleasure in praising you, because you have made us for yourself, and our heart is restless until it rests in you." [3] ReAwakening our lives for eternity will make us people who "truly live" without fear or regret of the temporal life. When William Wallace's life was coming to an end in the movie *Braveheart,* he said, "Every man dies, but not every man truly lives."

We were created for eternity, and as we grow in that identity, we become reflections of the power of that kingdom that attracts others to want to be citizens of eternity. Our lives today should reflect that eternal home. As Maximus said in the movie *Gladiator,* "What we do in this life echoes in eternity." Receiving eternal life gives us the power to leave a lasting legacy. Will we capture that moment?

A ReAwakening can only occur by faith alone in Jesus Christ. The Bible says it is impossible to please God without faith (Heb. 11:2). If we don't believe in something, it will never happen. When I was going to seminary, I was just about ready to drop out. I went to the little chapel in the middle of the school and asked God for help. I asked God to appear to me. I thought seminary was just too hard if God is not real. As I prayed, God began to fill my mind. I realized it wouldn't be just for Him to appear to me and not to appear to those who have gone before me. It is by faith and not by sight (2 Cor. 5:7), and more blessed are those who believe and have not seen (Jn. 20:29). This is the message I received: "How would I live my life if He did appear to me?"

How would you live your life if Jesus appeared to you? God wanted me to live my life by faith as if He had appeared to me. When we are faithless, He remains faithful, for He cannot deny himself (2 Tim. 2:13). Jesus cannot deny His perfect life that He has credited to us. Jesus tells us all you need is a mustard seed of faith (Matt. 17:20). Even with my tiny mustard seed of faith, I vowed to try to live the rest of my life as if He had appeared to me. He has appeared to me every day since. Always by faith. My faith has allowed me to believe that He will, in His timing, unleash a supernatural Reawakening.

I realized I experienced a lot of miraculous things from God. I define the miraculous as something God did in my life that was amazing but technically could still be explained away as being a coincidence. But by faith, I believed it was a miracle of God. Then I thought about what it means to experience the supernatural. I define the supernatural as something that breaks through the natural world and leaves no doubts that it was from God. What I call "A Road to Damascus Experience." I have never experienced the supernatural. God wanted me to live by faith as if the supernatural occurred in my life. I still desire to live a supernatural life like the early church. I still want God to appear to me supernaturally. But until it happens, I will patiently wait by faith on His perfect timing. What a Reawakening it will be!

The one thing that changed my life forever

was trusting the one life that made the most powerful eternal impact in this world. It was by faith in the supernatural life of Jesus, the death of Jesus, and the resurrection of Jesus. The greatest power the world has ever seen, the one life that revealed the greatest identity—the one man who left the greatest legacy, the real Superman. I believe in Him by faith, not by sight. That man's Good News of His life, death, and resurrection has ReAwakened a power in me to stand against the crises in our world and give me the hope that the supernatural power of God is still available for today. To have faith in our power-filled identity is vital for living a life of hope in the coming supernatural power of a ReAwakening. When we live by faith, the supernatural power will become a reality. To be Reawakened to a life of power that counts for eternity changes everything.

The Greatest Identity

If we are going to be ReAwakened to eternal life and leave the greatest legacy by living a power-filled identity, we must focus on the one who has already done it perfectly! This is called the Gospel (Good News). Whether you believe He is the King or not, I'm sure you at least know who He is. The calendar of all of human history is separated by His life and death (BC/AD). The greatest book ever written has been the number one bestseller every year since it was first produced, has been written in more languages, and has published more copies than any book in the history of the world, with no close seconds. It is all about His life, death, and resurrection, the very days that produced the most celebrated holidays in the world.

His teachings became the foundation for the United States of America. Fifty of the fifty-two signers of the Declaration of Independence believed in Him. The Pledge of Allegiance reflects loyalty and honor to Him. The book about His life became the foundation for the US Constitution, a book we must swear upon every time we take the witness stand in a court of law. All of America's money declares, "In God We Trust."

No one else in human history has caused more controversy. He was the greatest revolutionary the world has ever seen. Almost 2,000 years have passed, and He still has more followers than any other king in history. I am sure you know who I am talking about. **Any living, breathing, human being cannot deny that the one life that has impacted the world the most is the King, Jesus Christ! I believe the Father did this to leave no doubts about His Son.** In the movie *Pumping Iron,* Arnold Schwarzenegger's dream was to leave a legacy that lasted as long as Jesus Christ's, but even the Terminator couldn't deny His impact. The King says, "I'll be back" to prove He is the King of Kings. The entire foundation of this book lies in the identity of the King's life, death, and resurrection. If you do not believe Jesus is the King, I would recommend reading *More Than a Carpenter* by Josh McDowell and *The Case for Christ* by Lee Strobel. The factual evidence available to us is overwhelming.

This book is written on my educated assumption that the life of Jesus Christ has made the most powerful impact on the world. Nobody in their right mind can debate this fact. I am not asking you to follow Him, just that you make the simple factual declaration and, in doing so, be willing to look at the three things He did for us so we could enter eternity. Even Gandhi agreed: "If Christians would live like Jesus, then all India would be saved."

ReAwakening to our power-filled identity is rooted within the pages of the Bible. The Bible is considered our complete authority, God's perfect instruction to us that describes the concepts and blessings of our identity in Jesus Christ, which are revealed in the following scriptures:

- We are children of God (John 1:12)
- We are friends of Jesus (John 15:15)
- We are justified and redeemed (Romans 3:24)
- We are no longer slaves of sin (Romans 6:6)
- We are not condemned by God (Romans 8:1)
- We have been set free (Romans 8:2, Galatians 5:1)
- We are heirs of Christ (Romans 8:17)
- We have wisdom, righteousness, sanctification, and redemption (1 Corinthians 1:30)
- We are temples of the Holy Spirit (1 Corinthians 6:19)
- We are one Spirit with the Lord (1 Corinthians 6:17)
- We are victorious in Christ (2 Corinthians 2:14)
- We are new creations in Christ (2 Corinthians 5:17)
- We are the righteousness of Christ (2 Corinthians 5:21)
- We are one together in Christ (Galatians 3:28)
- We are blessed with every blessing (Ephesians 1:3)
- We are chosen of God (Ephesians 1:4)
- We are forgiven and redeemed (Ephesians 1:7)
- We are predestined to an inheritance (Ephesians 1:10-11)
- We are sealed with the Holy Spirit (Ephesians 1:13)

- We are made alive by Christ (Ephesians 2:4-5)
- We are seated with Christ (Ephesians 2:6)
- We are God's workmanship (Ephesians 2:10)
- We are righteous and holy (Ephesians 4:24)
- We are citizens of heaven (Philemon 3:20)
- We are complete in Christ (Colossians 2:10)
- We are raised up with Christ (Colossians 3:1)
- We are in Christ and share His glory (Colossians 3:4)
- We are holy and beloved (Colossians 3:12)
- We are His choice (1 Thessalonians 1:4)

Assuming such an identity exists, we would be crazy not to pursue it. As we pursue eternity, 2 Timothy 4:8 calls us to train toward godliness, a process 1 Corinthians 9 describes as training like an athlete. Like all living organisms, the church (the body of Christ) requires all its members to be healthy so it can reflect its new power (1 Cor. 12:12-27). Just as we use personal trainers to transform our physical bodies, the church must use a Spirit-driven power to train itself to grow the spiritual body (Eph. 4:11-16).

Receiving Eternal Life

The movie *The Matrix* parallels a foundational truth. We are slaves sold into bondage and the deceptions of the temporal worldly system. We have only two options: take a red pill that would open our eyes to the truth of the eternal we have been blinded to and see how deep the rabbit hole of deception really goes; or take the blue pill, put this book down, and continue to be deceived by the deceptions and lies of this temporal world.

I assume you took the red pill since you made it this far into the book. The journey we are about to take will change everything. Don't be surprised at just how deep that rabbit hole goes. It will astound you! Jesus makes a very bold statement in John 14:6: "I am the way, and the truth, and the life; no one comes to the Father but through Me." (Unless otherwise stated, all Scripture quotations are taken from the New American Standard Bible, NASB 95). With all the confusion of the worldly system with its thousands of different religions, tolerance, subjective and relativistic mindsets, belief systems, or acceptance of just about everything including sin, I know one thing for sure: Jesus is the way; Jesus is the truth; Jesus is the life, and no one goes to heaven apart from Him. This is the one truth I am willing to die for, not any manmade doctrine, not any religion or Christian denomination—only Jesus Christ.

Unfortunately, the Gospel has become corrupted and confused. If I ask ten pastors what the Gospel is, I will probably get ten different answers. Not only is the Gospel message confused, but few are living out its power. My biggest pet peeve is when Christians fight over truth. To debate and discuss truth is good, to fight and hate over truth is bad. The biggest factor in determining if someone is walking in the power of the Gospel is rooted in the word *love*. Without love, we just become noisy and clanging preachers (1 Cor. 13:1). Christians who are finite should stand in awe and reverence of God's infinite word. No person has a monopoly on God's infinite truth.

When I was at seminary, I got frustrated in theology class about how many Christians were fighting over the doctrines of the Bible. I realized that is the normal outcome of our fallen human nature when trying to understand the infinite depths of God's word. Instead of being confused, I rejoiced. I thought how amazing it is for the most brilliant theological minds to struggle and fight over the truth of the Bible. The Bible is infinitely more than any finite creature will ever be able to understand. Of course, the fallen nature will be confused about God's infinite and holy word. The Bible says this in 1 Corinthians 13:12-13:

> *For now, we see in a mirror dimly, but then face to face; now I know in part, but then I will know fully just as I also have been fully known. But now faith, hope, love, abide these three; but the greatest of these is love.*

Without love, we have no power. I see so many pastors and theologians speak as if they have a monopoly on biblical truth. They are conceited, arrogant, boastful, and argumentative, without any reflection of the fruit of the Spirit, particularly love. God is love, and if we don't love, we don't have the Spirit of God within us. 1 John 2:3-6 states this:

> *By this we know that we have come to know Him, if we keep His commandments. The one who says, "I have come to know Him," and does not keep His commandments, is a liar, and the truth is not in him; but whoever keeps His word, in him the love of God has truly*

*been perfected. By this we know that
we are in Him: the one who says he
abides in Him ought himself to walk
in the same manner as He walked.*

The Great Commandment is still the Greatest Commandment. The Great Commandment in Matthew 22:35-40 calls us to love God and love people. The Gospel is the greatest message of love the world has ever seen. The Father sending His one and only Son to die for our sins is the greatest picture of love. I have three children, and I would never let any of them suffer and die for anyone. But our Father loved the world so much, He sent us His one and only Son, His baby sent to us in a manger. 1 John 3:16-18 defines love for us:

*We know love by this, that He laid down
His life for us; and we ought to lay down
our lives for the brethren. But whoever has
the world's goods, and sees his brother
in need and closes his heart against him,
how does the love of God abide in him?
Little children, let us not love with word
or with tongue, but in deed and truth.*

Yet some Christians let their superior theological knowledge destroy other Christians. Love builds up, but knowledge puffs up and makes us arrogant (1 Cor. 8:1). Using our correct theological knowledge at the expense of hurting other Christians is not love. Without love, there is no Gospel power. We who are mature and have a strong theological knowledge ought to love the brethren to the truth (Eph. 4:15). We also should stop playing the role of the Holy Spirit; the Holy Spirit is the one who convicts and leads people to the truth. Romans 14:4-13, 22 sums up the entire point I am trying to convey:

> *Who are you to judge the servant of another? To his own master he stands or falls; and he will stand, for the Lord is able to make him stand. One person regards one day above another, another regards every day alike. Each person must be fully convinced in his own mind. He who observes the day, observes it for the Lord, and he who eats, does so for the Lord, for he gives thanks to God; and he who eats not, for the Lord he does not eat, and gives thanks to God. For not one of us lives for himself, and not one dies for himself; for if we live, we live for the Lord, or if we die, we die for the Lord; therefore, whether we live or die, we are the Lord's. For to this end Christ died and lived again, that He might be Lord both of the dead and of the living. But you, why do you judge your brother? Or you again, why do you regard your brother with contempt? For we will all stand before the judgment seat of God. For it is written, "As I live, says the Lord, every knee shall bow to Me, And every tongue shall give praise to God." So, then each one of us will give an account of himself to God. Therefore, let us not judge one another anymore, but rather determine this—not to put an obstacle or a stumbling block in a brother's way. The faith which you have, have as your own conviction before God. Happy is he who does not condemn himself in what he approves.*

It breaks my heart to see some incredible Christian teachers destroy their witness for the Lord because they hold to their truth over His love. The love of God is what changes hearts. Not our correct doctrine and theology. Correct theology is so desperately needed, but without love, we are nothing (1 Cor. 13:2). *Nothing* in the Greek means nothing. It seems so simple, but our sinful natures make it very difficult. We would rather force our theological truth on people rather than to just love them to the truth. Just meditate on this and think about it for a while. An old saying I heard was, "people don't care how much you know until they know how much you care." Jesus says the whole Bible is summed up by this: love God and love people (Matt. 22:40). The root of the Gospel is the love of God and people.

Having said that, the following presentation lays down the book's foundation. It is of foremost importance. The Bible says God is holy, which means He is perfect and separate from any kind of sin (Lev. 11:44; 1 Pet. 1:16). Sin is anything that is not perfect. God is perfect (without sin), and heaven is a perfect place (without sin). God cannot be in the midst of sin. I am sure we all would agree with Romans 3:23 that there are no perfect people, for "All have sinned and fall short of the glory of God." If sin were to enter heaven, it would be destroyed by God's holiness.

Every soul upon the earth has a serious problem because perfection is required to live forever in heaven with God. Unfortunately, many simply think God judges us too strictly. We have drifted away from God's standards and base goodness and righteousness on human standards. As a result, many believe they're already in right standing with

God because they're "good people" or "better than a lot of people" they know. However, that is the wrong standard because the Bible says only God is good. Our sins only serve to create a gap between God and us.

Mankind has been under God's condemnation since the first man rebelled against God and brought sin into the world (Rom. 5:12). As a result, all are guilty of sin (Rom. 5:18). The punishment for sin is physical and spiritual death (Rom. 6:23) followed by an eternity in a place of punishment and separation from God (Rev. 20:15, Matt. 25:46). This is also called the "second death" (Rev. 20:14–15). That's the bad news.

The Good News is God loves us and wants us to spend eternity with Him. His great love made a way for people to be ReAwakened, to be made holy, to be forgiven of their sins, and to be resurrected to a power-filled identity by sending His Son, Jesus Christ, to live, die, and be resurrected to a new life. Jesus lived a perfect life, and He did it for us. God placing our sins on Christ ensures that all who believe in Jesus's perfect life that He credits to us, His death that paid the penalty for all our sins, and His resurrection that assures us that the same Spirit who raised Jesus to new life, will also ReAwaken us to new life with Him forever.

This is the best news anyone will ever hear, and what you do with this news will determine where you spend eternity. Remember, only those who place their faith in the life, death, and resurrection of Jesus Christ will go to heaven when they die (Acts 4:12, Col. 1:14). God is calling you to choose life. To do so, you must first admit that you have rebelled against God and that you are a sinner who needs a Savior. Then you just call upon the name of the Lord to be saved (Rom. 10:13). If you would like to do that, simply pray the following:

> *God, I realize that perfection is required for heaven. I believe no one else is holy and perfect except You. I also admit that I am not perfect, that I am a sinner in need of forgiveness. Right now, I accept that Jesus Christ lived a perfect life on my behalf and died on the cross to forgive me of all my past, present, and future sins. I also believe that He was buried in a tomb and raised on the third day, and the same Spirit who raised Jesus from the dead will raise me to new spiritual life both now and in the future when I will receive my new, glorified body. I turn from my sinful disobedience and turn to Jesus to be the King and Savior of my life. I receive Jesus Christ into my heart as my personal Lord and Savior. I believe, God; help me with my doubts. In Jesus's name. Amen.*

Why We Need a ReAwakening

Why do we need a ReAwakening? The answer lies in the fact of the evil and crises in our world today. We need to ReAwaken a strength and power within us to be able to survive the crises of this world and overcome the evil one.

As you read, keep in mind the question I always ask everyone I meet; "Have you found anything worth dying for? What are you willing to die for?" When you are willing to die, it frees you to ReAwaken in power. The Bible says when you are willing to die, you will ReAwaken to a new power-filled identity (Rom. 7:4-6). A lot of people will die for family, friends, and spouses. Would you still die for your family, friends, and spouse when they betray you? When they cheat on you? When they stab you in the back? When they hate you? The Bible teaches us that there is only one who will never fail us. This life is hard, plain and simple. If you never find the one who is worthy to die for, you will never know what it means to truly ReAwaken in power. To be able to survive the worst crisis imaginable in this life, you must know the

Why We Need a ReAwakening

one who is worth dying for and has the power to ReAwaken again from the dead.

Imagine being separated from anything that is good, forever. The Bible says that only God is good. Please bear with me during the next few paragraphs. Please don't close this book. I know it will be easy for you to shut me out and get angry with me because of the bad news I am going to present. Before you can understand the depths of the Good News, you must understand the depths of the bad news—the reason we need a Reawakening.

What if I called you a sinner and said you are destined to be separated from anything that is good? How would you respond? Probably not too favorably. What if I said every human being that has ever been born is a sinner and destined for hell? Hell is simply separation from a good God. You may not like that very much. What if I was telling you the truth? The question becomes, would you want to know the truth? Jack Nicholson once said in the movie *A Few Good Men,* "You can't handle the truth." In the movie *The Matrix,* Neo was given two options: take a blue pill and go right back to *your* truth, or take the red pill and see how far the rabbit hole of truth really goes. The red pill will reveal the truth of our sinful state and the reality of hell. The bad news!

We may not like the terms "hell" and "sinner," especially if we connect those terms to evil, murderers, and child molesters. But we must understand what the Bible means by these terms and remove our presuppositional thoughts about those terms. Let's look at what the Bible teaches.

The Bible says that God is absolutely holy and that all who do not match His perfect moral standard are "sinners," a term that simply means *missing God's perfect standard.* If we sin to any degree, we become something other than what God intended us to be. That means even stealing a cookie when your mom wasn't looking. That is stealing. God has given us His Holy Law to reveal our sinful condition. Maybe we have been angry with someone; the Bible says that anger is as bad as murder. Or, we wanted something someone else possessed; that is covetousness. We could have lusted after a person; the Bible says that it is as bad as adultery. Have we disrespected our parents? Have we ever said God's name in vain? Have we ever loved something more than God? Have we failed to keep one day a week holy? Have we ever loved or worship a material thing? There are an estimated 613 commandments, and we have broken just the first ten. We are in big trouble according to God's Law. We still have 603 more commandments to go. We are lying, murdering, adulterous, covetous, blaspheming, lusting, sabbath-breaking, dishonoring our parents, idol-worshiping idolaters. You still want to read my book? Romans 7:7–13 speaks of the purpose of God's Law:

> *What shall we say then? Is the Law sin? May it never be! On the contrary, I would not have come to know sin except through the Law; for I would not have known about coveting if the Law had not said, "You shall not covet." But sin, taking opportunity through the commandment, produced in*

Why We Need a ReAwakening   23

me coveting of every kind; for apart from the Law sin is dead. I was once alive apart from the Law; but when the commandment came, sin became alive and I died; and this commandment, which was to result in life, proved to result in death for me; for sin, taking an opportunity through the commandment, deceived me and through it killed me. So then, the Law is holy, and the commandment is holy and righteous and good. Therefore, did that which is good become a cause of death for me? May it never be! Rather it was sin, in order that it might be shown to be sin by effecting my death through that which is good, so that through the commandment sin would become utterly sinful.

God created us in His image (Rom. 3:23; Jas. 2:10). He made us to reflect His holy nature (1 Pet. 1:16). Our sins not only hurt us but also separate us from a relationship with a holy God (Eph. 4:30). If our sin is not dealt with, we are destined to a place separated from a holy God called Hell. I have already proven that I am a sinner by breaking the first ten commandments right out of the gate, as mentioned above. You may say God judges us too hard. This would be an incorrect assertion. God cannot change His holy nature. He is Who He is! The name for God Yahweh means "I am, who I am." Perfect and holy. Anything that falls short of His perfect moral nature is naturally classified by the Bible as a sinner (Rom. 3:32). Holy means separate from sin. God cannot be in the presence of sin, for His holy nature would consume anything that is not holy. I might make you very angry by taking this a step further. God says if you are not holy (perfect), you can't go to heaven. Therefore, all those who are not perfect like God will be condemned and separated to a place called Hell. How can God require me to be perfect? That is simply not fair! Let's examine this further.

If we truly looked deep within ourselves, we will see that our own sinful nature declares the truth of God's word. We are self-focused, angry, greedy, arrogant, and seek our own good before we ever seek the good of others... if we ever do. We focus on us first, then maybe on our families, and then maybe on God. We see the world from our selfish inner-focused perspective. We are natural-born sinners! Paul says it like this in Romans 3:10-18:

> *There is no one righteous, not even one, there is no one who understands, there is no one who seeks God. All have turned away, together they have become worthless; there is no one who shows kindness, not even one. Their throats are open graves, they deceive with their tongues, the poison of asps is under their lips. Their mouths are full of cursing and bitterness. Their feet are swift to shed blood, ruin and misery are in their paths, and the way of peace they have not known. There is no fear of God before their eyes.*

We all fall short of God's standards in His economy, in His heavenly kingdom. We must not compare ourselves to the world's standards or other people. For only God is good. The above text states, "There is no one who understands, there is no one who seeks God." If this is the case, no one can understand or seek God without an incredible act of God's mercy and grace in ReAwakening our hearts with a new Spirit. Jesus provided a way for us to be ReAwakened almost two thousand years ago. The more we drift away from that powerful event, the more our world needs a Reawakening. This is done by God's Spirit regenerating us to come to life from the dead and crucify the old identity through faith in His new power-filled identity (Col. 2:13), an identity that has the power for us to live as God originally intended, in His image. It is done by putting our faith completely in Jesus Christ. Yet some Christians do not understand their power-filled identity in Christ and need a Reawakening. Christians sometimes display the very thing that Christ stood against. How can Christians who know they are sinners and nothing but filthy rags judge anyone? How can Christians, who know they were dead and buried in their sins and transgressions and have been brought to life again by the gracious hand of God, look down upon anyone?

Christians have been saved by a free gift called grace. It comes from our faith in Christ alone and not by anything we do (Eph. 2:8-9). It is not about what we do but about what Christ has done. Our identity is rooted in this Good News to share with others. This is the identity of Jesus Christ who came to save us and not condemn us, according to John 3:16-17 (NET): "For this is the way God loved the world: He gave His one and only Son, so that everyone who believes in Him will not perish but have eternal life. For God did not send

His Son into the world to condemn the world, but that the world should be saved through Him." If Jesus didn't come to judge and condemn, what right do followers have to judge and condemn?

The bad news is that we all fall short of God's glory. Yet, we see so many so-called Christians judging and condemning homosexuals, those who had an abortion, anyone who sins. This is not the calling of a Christian. We are called to share the Good News. Those who don't believe in Christ don't have the Holy Spirit who can lead them into all truth. We spend our time wasting our breath by protesting those who can't believe what we believe without the Holy Spirit. The Holy Spirit's job is to convict and lead people to repentance and the truth. We must share the Gospel and make sure they have the Holy Spirit. Christians must stop playing the role of the Holy Spirit. We must understand the bad news to be Reawakened with a power-filled identity that comes from understanding the power of the Good News. If Christians understood the power of the Gospel, they would stop condemning and judging and start sharing the Gospel. When we understand the bad news, we will not judge but will tell others about the one who can save them. For there is no condemnation for those who are in Christ Jesus (Rom. 8:1). The world already knows it stands condemned (Jn. 3:18-19). We are not called to bring more condemnation by judging those who know they are condemned. We are called to fulfill the Great Commission by bringing Good News.

Our world continues to deceive us into thinking God is unfair. It tells us the goal of life is to get as much as we can while we can and avoid pain at all costs. It teaches us to build a name for ourselves, to seek fame and fortune, to seek popularity, because Satan's kingdom finds its identity in status, wealth, and success. C. S. Lewis reflects in *The Screwtape Letters* on this false identity: "Prosperity knits a man to the world. He feels that he is 'finding his place in it,' while really it is finding its place in him. His increasing reputation, his widening circle or acquaintances, his sense of importance, the growing pressure of absorbing and agreeable work, build up in him a sense of being really at home in earth." [4]

A ReAwakening

With all the unbelief in our world today, I am surprised God works at all. Living in a skeptical, relativistic, and subjective culture, and in an existential postmodern world, the only way we are going to convince others of the Gospel is by living out the power of the Gospel. We must reflect the power of the Gospel in our lives as witnesses of the resurrected Christ in us. Paul clearly says in 1 Corinthians 4:20, "For the kingdom of God does not consist in words but in power." If we are going to transform this world for Jesus Christ, we must live out the power of His Gospel. The Gospel not only saves us, but it is also our example of how we should live. It's the only way kingdom-empowered people can lead others to a transformation that will last for eternity!

Former Dallas Theological Seminary professor Jack Deere boldly teaches about the power of the Holy Spirit in his book *Surprised by the Power of the Spirit.* He mentions that anything that drives away the presence of the King, such as apostasy, legalism, and unbelief, will drive away the presence of the kingdom power, though I choose the word "idolatry" instead of "apostasy." Deere came from a very conservative seminary, and God revealed the power that was our divine inheritance to him.

The first weapon Satan uses is unbelief. This is an attack on the mind against the Great Commandment. If we don't believe the Gospel, Satan has won. We remain dead and buried in our sins. Satan also doesn't want the church to believe in its God-given power-filled identity. Here we see the focus of this book. The Gospel not only saves us, but it is also our example of how to live. Without faith in the power of God in our lives, we will never experience all that God has prepared for those who love Him. Satan uses unbelief to stop our faith and knowledge of the Lord Jesus Christ. If we don't believe in Him, we will not act. Before you turn your belief away from the supernatural power of God's kingdom, ask yourself whether you really ever had faith in it. How many times have you prayed for the supernatural to occur in your life and ministry? It is impossible to please God without faith (Heb. 11:6). Imagine if we had faith in God to work powerfully through us; we would fear nothing, and nothing would be impossible for us. If we keep our eyes on Jesus, we will be able to walk on water, figuratively. Walk above all the evil and crises.

One important note: we cannot allow our experiences to depict the reality of the King and His kingdom. Read the four Gospels very carefully and see how the King blesses the faith of those who believe in the King and His kingdom power. Deere comments: "The surprising thing to me today is not how little God heals among the conservative evangelical church, but that he heals at all. So much of the church is so filled with unbelief that I am truly amazed that anyone ever gets healed." [5] We can take that one step further; today, our world has such little faith in the power of God, I am surprised that we ever see God work at all. Can the church at least consider the possibility that Jesus has prepared such an incredible Gospel-empowered identity that we haven't even begun to touch on yet? Would it be that crazy to believe in the supernatural power of the King and His kingdom? Our journey to experiencing this supernatural power begins with humbling ourselves and acknowledging we have become an unbelieving people. Our faith will then lead us to a Reawakening.

The second weapon Satan uses is idolatry and has always been a major problem among the people of God. This is a direct attack on the heart of the Great Commandment. Satan continues to entice us to eat the fruit of his kingdom: sex, drugs, money, fame, and popularity. These things feel really good at first, just like a drug, but like the addiction, the end results are devastating. The world can never fill your heart with what it longs for. We were created for eternity and the kingdom of God. You can try to fill that God-shaped hole in your heart with the things of this world, but the more you get, the more you want. Loving God is the foundation, but Satan will entice us to love the world. John tells us that if you love the world, the love of God is not in you (1 Jn. 2:15).

Unfortunately, even people in America, a country that God blessed because it was built on Christian foundations, are trying to find rest in any number of other religions and best-selling self-help books. And we wonder why most conservative evangelical churches are dying. The church has also moved from being a powerful organism to becoming a worldly business organization that only holds onto a form of godliness, denying its true power. The church was created to influence the world, yet the world is influencing the church. It's because idolatry is running rampant in our churches. Idolatry is the second weapon of the enemy to defeat a heart of repentance (this will be discussed in detail later). Homosexuals are being allowed to be pastors, and secular self-help programs are being taught in churches instead of the Word of God. Numbers and conversions have become the priority over making disciples. My own denomination is more concerned with how many baptisms we performed, instead of how many disciples we have made.

One thing that has absolutely angered me as a pastor for the past twenty years is the so-called TV evangelists who promise God will bless those who sow a seed of money in their ministry. Or maybe they promise to send you a fifty-cent bottle of prayer oil if you send them a hundred dollars. This is called greed, and Paul talks about this form of idolatry in Colossians 3:5. Anything that takes away from the glory of the King is from the kingdom of this world.

The false-prosperity gospel teachers, who declare that prosperity is necessary for completing the Lord's work, are plaguing America's churches. So how do they explain that Jesus and the apostles had nothing and were put to death for their faith? That doesn't sound too prosperous. Forgive me for my sarcasm and harsh words toward this movement, but proponents of the prosperity gospel claim that Jesus was wealthy and wore all the latest designer clothes of His day. What a dangerous teaching, to take away from the suffering of our Lord, as He had nowhere to even lay His head. Jesus suffered through poverty for you and me. To take that part of His suffering away from Him takes on a form of blasphemy. Anything exalted above the Father, the Son, and the Holy Spirit is idolatry. Watch out for the idolatry of greed; it will drive away the presence and power of God's kingdom.

We must humble ourselves and acknowledge that we have become an idolatrous people if we're ever to see a visible ReAwakening of the manifestations of the power of the kingdom of God that the first-century church saw. Instead, we come up with every theological idea in the world that says the supernatural was only for the first-century Christians to verify and establish the church. We might as well say the power of God has ceased in our world today. How foolish, how blind we have become to the obvious truth that lies before us.

Legalism is the final attack that our churches are plagued with, the third weapon of the enemy. Legalism is an attack on our hope in our resurrection power. Satan attacks the soul of the Great

Commandment and removes the power to live a godly life in Jesus Christ. Satan does whatever he can to get us to depend on our strength, to trust in the religious activity, the church programs, and the power of man instead of the power of the King and His kingdom. That's the core of legalism. In essence, we take God's glory away by claiming the power and influence of the church is not from God, but from the church. The Old Testament gives us so many insights into and instructions about what not to do, beginning with Isaiah 29:13-14 (ESV):

> *"And the Lord said: 'Because this people draw near with their mouth and honor me with their lips, while their hearts are far from me, and their fear of me is a commandment taught by men, therefore, behold, I will again do wonderful things with this people, with wonder upon wonder; and the wisdom of their wise men shall perish, and the discernment of their discerning men shall be hidden.'"*

God would have nothing to do with legalistic Israel. Because they took God's glory for themselves, God would blind them to the coming King and His kingdom power. The Israelites' legalistic form of religion drove the presence and power of the King out of the nation. Paul talked about this with young Timothy in 2 Timothy 3:1-9 (ESV):

> *"But understand this, that in the last days there will come times of difficulty. For people will be lovers of self, lovers of money, proud, arrogant, abusive, disobedient to their parents, ungrateful,*

unholy, heartless, unappeasable, slanderous, without self-control, brutal, not loving good, treacherous, reckless, swollen with conceit, lovers of pleasure rather than lovers of God, having the appearance of godliness, but denying its power. Avoid such people. For among them are those who creep into households and capture weak women, burdened with sins and led astray by various passions, always learning and never able to arrive at a knowledge of the truth."

You will never find rest for your soul until it rests in the King. Many people wonder why they feel so restless, why they feel as if they are constantly spinning their wheels, why life seems meaningless and purposeless. Until you rest in Jesus, you will never ReAwaken to your God-given power.

The Israelites wanted the Messiah on their terms; as a result, they were blinded to the wisdom of God and never arrived at a knowledge of the truth. Eventually, God turned from Israel and turned to the church. We must be careful not to be simply hearers of His Word, but doers. We need more than a knowledge of God; God wants our hearts. As we move out as doers of His Word, we must always give Him the glory for His power and grace that work through us, for apart from Him, we can do nothing.

The power of the King and His kingdom comes through those who love the King with all their hearts, all their minds, and all their souls. Satan uses unbelief, idolatry, and legalism as a direct attack on the power of the Holy Spirit in our lives. Our objective is to be so consumed with the King that Christ to the world is all we are. When we know the King, we live out the Great Commandment and fulfill the Great Commission by loving the King, and we reflect the King in resurrection power. Working together, the three levels of a power-filled identity—mind/knowing/personal, heart/love/relational, and soul/power/missional—produce holistic disciples who have no room for unbelief, idolatry, and legalism.

God isn't looking for perfect people but humble and surrendered people. The eyes of the Lord go to and from throughout the earth looking to strengthen hearts that are fully committed to Him (2 Chron. 16:9). That means being honest and humbling ourselves in the presence of the King. If God's people would do this, God would bring His kingdom, as He says in 2 Chronicles 7:14:

> *"And if My people who are called by My name humble themselves and pray and seek My face and turn from their wicked ways, then I will hear from heaven, will forgive their sin and will heal their land."*

The constant battle between the kingdom of Satan and the kingdom of God rages war within all of us. Ecclesiastes 3:11 teaches that God has written eternity on our hearts, and our souls will not rest until it rests in the King. Man was created to enjoy the King and His kingdom power, not to pursue all the pleasures of this world that leave us empty. Once we engage Satan's way of fulfillment, the results are always a lack of power, death, emptiness, and destruction. The deceiver wants to hurt us, harm us, and even get us to jump off a bridge if he can. The path to ReAwakening our power-filled identity starts with understanding what the Bible says about the origin of the one who stole our identity.

Let's start at the beginning, not my beginning, but the beginning that explains how our identity was stolen and explains why we exist.

Why Are We Here?

Back to Eternity Past

We are here to participate in "The Greatest Story Ever Told" by reflecting God's glory to a fallen world. We are here to be reflectors of God's glory. To declare the glory of God to the earthly realm and the heavenly realm (Eph. 3:9-10). The question becomes, why would God need anyone or anything to declare His glory? The answer is because He loves us and wants us to experience His glory fully.

How does this happen? He does this through parables (stories). To understand the depths of the wisdom of God, God likes to use stories to convey deeper spiritual truths. The Father and Jesus are just alike and tell parables to bring out these truths. I call this "The Greatest Story Ever Told." This is the greatest spiritual truth. God allows us to become one with Him through His Son Jesus Christ as God reflects His glory through our lives. I don't know of a better way to know someone than to watch their life and power manifest itself through our lives. Satan and one-third of the angels didn't know the greatness of the glory of God, so they rebelled against Him. This time around, God lives in us, so we have no questions about His greatness. The book of Ephesians calls this an incredible mystery. In Colossians 1:27, Paul states it perfectly:

> *"To whom God willed to make known what is the riches of the glory of this mystery among the Gentiles, which is Christ in you, the hope of glory."*

The most powerful being, the God of all creation, lives in those who believe. I've been a Christian for over forty years and can't quite fathom this amazing grace. God is in me and God is in you! There can be no greater love, no greater gift than to become one with our creator.

Let's take a journey together and learn how "The Greatest Story Ever Told" allows us to Re-Awaken to a legacy in this life that will count for eternity. It starts by knowing the whole story. Instead of going "back to the future," as a popular movie suggests, we are going to go back to eternity past, beginning with two important chapters in the Bible that answer the questions, "Why am I here?" and "Why do I exist?" Those are Ezekiel 28 and Isaiah 14, both of which take us back to the beginning before the earth was formed. As we look to these prophetic texts of the Old Testament, we will observe how Scripture interpreting Scripture puts all the pieces of the puzzle together. I cover this in greater detail in my book *Identity Crisis* but will cover it briefly now. Just as we can confirm other prophecies through Scripture, we can confirm the prophecies of Ezekiel 28 and Isaiah 14 as references to Satan.

Let's assume these two texts refer to Satan. If so, then the first sin ever committed was in eternity past before God ever laid the foundation of the world. The texts are prophecies concerning evil earthly kings. But in any prophecy, there may be a double fulfillment, such as the prophecies of Emmanuel and the Suffering Servant seen in the book of Isaiah. It is safe to say both those prophecies could have been fulfilled in Isaiah's time, but the New Testament informs us of a deeper fulfillment, a double fulfillment seen in the life of Christ. These prophecies could have been fulfilled by the earthly kings, but as we read deeper into the text, we begin to realize they couldn't have fulfilled all these prophecies. When a prophet prophesied over someone, he would begin prophesying about the root of the evil behind the earthly person. The prophet would take a peripheral view and look into the cause of the evil.

These texts are obviously not describing human kings. But transitions from "ruler" to "king" demonstrates a deeper prophetic event that looks to a sinister puppet master who influences the strings of the evil kings. The mention of the Garden of Eden begins to suggest there is obviously a deeper influence. The prophecies reveal Satan, who was the puppet master of the earthly evil kings, the true king of darkness who was motivating the human kings. As we look at all the evil rulers throughout history (Alexander the Great, Herod the Great, Genghis Khan, Mussolini, Hit-

Why Are We Here?

ler, etc.), we can see the spirit of the Antichrist deceiving and influencing these leaders. In light of the divine revelation of Scripture, we can conclude that Satan was in the Garden of Eden (Gen. 3:1-7), and his sin was pride (1 Tim. 3:6). He also dwelled in God's presence (Job 1:6-12). God both judges the human king of Tyre for his pride (Ezek. 28:1-10), and the satanic "king" of Tyre for his pride (vv. 11-19). The king of Tyre was tempted and deceived by the same sin as Satan and would suffer the same fate. Just a coincidence?

Ezekiel described the origin of Satan as God originally created him (vv. 12-15a). He was *the model of perfection, full of wisdom, and perfect in beauty*. God created Satan as a beautiful angel (Lucifer) that would reflect His glory to the entire angelic realm. But even though God gave Lucifer an exalted place in heaven, ultimately, He cast him down to *Eden, the garden of God*, God's new creation on earth, paradise (Gen. 2:8-14). In the Old Testament, stones are used at times to describe a reflection: *every precious stone adorned* him. The nine precious stones symbolized Lucifer's beauty and high position of reflecting God's glory to the angelic realm. Now, God created man in His image to become a new reflection of God's glory. So, in essence, because of Lucifer's rebellion, God replaced Lucifer with man as a new reflector. Because God is just, He will also replace man if he rebels.

God had placed Lucifer at His right hand to be the bright morning star that reflected His glory to all the angels *as a guardian cherub*. The cherubim were the angels who walked with God and in the midst of His holiness. Lucifer also met with God at His *holy mountain*, heaven, and he *walked among the fiery stones*. Ezekiel was stating that Lucifer had access to God's presence. Adam and Eve also had access to God's presence as they walked and talked with Him in the Garden of Eden. Sin separates us from the presence of God and a relationship with God. Satan wasn't too happy to be replaced by man. The same thing that got Satan kicked out of heaven is the same temptation Satan used to get Adam and Eve kicked out of the Garden: "You will be like God" (Gen. 3:5). God is a just God and will always act just and fair. Satan knew of God's justice as he reflected that justice throughout eternity. Now Satan hates God and man for trying to replace him. Now the battle rages on in "The Greatest Story Ever Told" that unfolds on the stage of the earth. And we have the opportunity to be the heroes of "The Greatest Story Ever Told" by putting our trust in the King.

Lucifer's sin resulted in his being cast out from the presence of God *from the mount of God*. Lucifer rebelled against God in heaven and was cast down to the earth to be the leading villain in The Greatest Story Ever Told (Lk. 10:18). The entire angelic realm, and creation itself, could never fathom the depths and splendor of the glory of God. Therefore, God presents a story (parable) to all creation to reveal the greatness of His glory that unfolds on the stage of the earth. The theme of the story is that Lucifer, a created being, had no right to think he could be the God of all creation by rebelling against Him.

The plot of the story is to reveal the greatness of God. God casts Satan to earth to play god ("god of the air"; "prince of this world"), and then God simply breathes into the dust of the earth to overcome the so-called god (Thess. 2:7-11). God creates a new reflector who would be able to overcome Lucifer simply by faith in the greatness of God. Satan wanted to be God, through pride, but if a human being would simply trust and submit to the sovereign creator of everything by humbling himself or herself, God would highly exalt humanity (Js. 4:10, 1 Pet. 5:6) to become the very thing Lucifer wanted: to be like God—but by humility, not pride. When we humble ourselves before the one who has no equal, not even a close second, God allows us to be partakers of His glory and plan (Jn. 17:22-23) by becoming children of God, and thus we are (1 Jn. 3:1). And what an identity it is!

A thorough look at the Bible seems to reveal that Satan must have sinned and fallen, which explains why an already-sinister being existed in God's good creation account in Genesis. Otherwise, without the origin of Satan falling to the earth, the conundrum of a bad serpent existing in a good creation is unresolved. The systematic study of the Bible seems to declare a harmony of the Ezekiel and Isaiah texts that give strong support to the account of the origin of Satan. As we continue the story of Adam and Eve, the support only grows stronger.

The introduction of the serpent in Genesis 3 reveals the depths of Satan's fight for our souls and His kingdom of darkness on earth. Again, we are faced with a major biblical conundrum in Genesis 3:1; if the aforementioned texts of Ezekiel and Isaiah are not an explanation of the previously fallen intelligence to the world, then where did this serpent come from? God created everything good, and it is obvious from the text itself that this serpent is bad; it is obviously already focused on evil purposes that defy the sovereign rule of God on earth.

Who was the serpent? Again, as previously discussed, the root of all evil lies in the person of Satan. By the authority of the New Testament, we find the serpent is indeed Satan (Jn. 8:44, Rev. 12:9, Rom. 16:20, 1 Cor. 10:20). With this as our backdrop, remember Ezekiel 28:11-19 and Isaiah 14:12-17. Watch how these texts directly line up with the tactics of the serpent. Satan knew God is a just God and that if he was kicked out of heaven for wanting to be God, then God would kick his own man and woman out of paradise if they wanted to be God. The very thing that got Satan kicked out of heaven was the very temptation he used to get Adam and Eve kicked out of paradise. He became very bold in Genesis 3:4-5 when he said to the woman, "You surely will not die! For God knows that in the day you eat from it your eyes will be opened, and you will be like God, knowing good and evil."

In essence, Satan whispered, "God doesn't want you to be like Him because you will become a threat to Him." Watch closely, the insanity of the first sin. Lucifer got tired of being the second-hand man reflecting God's glory throughout eternity to the whole angelic realm. Then Satan keeps looking up to the throne of God, thinking there is only one above him. He looks up to God and sees the King of Kings, invincible in battle, undefeatable, omnipotent, the almighty. Then he says, "I think I can take Him." Don't miss the humor in Satan's misunderstanding of the glory and greatness of God. No created being will ever be a threat to the Lord our God Most High. Satan revealed a false identity to Eve by getting her to believe that God's threat of death was a lie because he wanted Eve to become the god of her own world. Notice the little *g* in god. We can play God but by no means will we ever be able to compare to God. At that point, Eve had a choice between God's given identity or the false identity presented by the serpent. Her choice was devastating to all mankind. She then proceeded to give the fruit to Adam, and they chose the false identity for all humanity.

Satan always tempts people to choose his false identity by making them think they can be "like God," even if it is through the king of Tyre (Ezek. 28:11) or the king of Babylon (Isa. 14:12). Pride always goes before the fall. Satan wants us all to become gods of our own world so we can "fall" straight to hell with him. In a sense, what Satan said came true; they became like a god (Gen. 3:22). What seems good at the beginning can produce death in the end—just like drugs. Satan wants to kill and destroy God's children, and he will lie and deceive to achieve that end. And that is exactly what he did when he said, "You surely will not die!" Adam was created mortal but could have lived forever in the presence of God. But God's Word always holds true: "But from the tree of the knowledge of good and evil you shall not eat, for in the day that you eat from it you will surely die" (Gen. 2:17). Adam brought not only physical death to humanity on that day but also spiritual death; just as God had said, he spiritually died on that very day. As a result, man lost his true identity in God. From Adam and Eve's disobedience, a great divide was established between man and God because God is holy, perfect, and separated from sin. Because the first man chose to listen to the deception of the satanic king, his sin separated him from his position with God, just like Satan's did. All men and women from this point inherit what is called theologically "Total Depravity." We have been imputed with the first fathers' sin, and we now need someone to ReAwaken and save us from the death-producing sin. Only the salvation work of the Savior could accomplish such a mission. As Romans 5:18-19 states:

> *Then as through one transgression there resulted condemnation to all men, even so through one act of righteousness there resulted justification of life to all men. For as through the one man's disobedience the many were made sinners, even so through the obedience of the One the many will be made righteous.*

The fall created not only spiritual death but also physical death. Man became subject to sickness, disease, deformity, bodily death, and crises. In other words, the world became cursed with an *Identity Crisis*. Women were cursed with pain in childbirth and given kingdom dependence to rule

Why Are We Here?

over the man. The earth was cursed, and man had to till the ground to make a living. Because man followed Satan's rebellion against God's kingdom, Satan was able to confuse the rule of God's kingdom identity, man lost his kingdom authority, and the worldly system began a false identity. Satan tricked the world into believing the worldly system can provide fulfillment. God's holiness should drive us to our knees, and we must cry out to him for help.

God wants to ReAwaken us with our God-given identity, as Exodus 29:45-46 teaches:

"I will dwell among the sons of Israel and will be their God. They shall know that I am the LORD their God who brought them out of the land of Egypt, that I might dwell among them; I am the LORD their God."

God wants us to know He is King of all and that there are no close seconds. We must understand the depths of His glory revealed through His love, mercy, and grace before we can reflect His kingdom glory. The irony is that the very thing Satan wanted, to become like God, to be a reflector of God's glory, can be ours through humility, not pride. Pride always goes before the fall. When we humble ourselves and acknowledge there is no one like our God and there is nothing we can do to save ourselves, an incredible transformation takes place. We must continue to cry out as Moses did. "God, show us your glory!"

Throughout the pages of the Bible, "The Greatest Story Ever Told," God is making sure His purposes are clearly understood this time around.

God alone is holy. We all fall short of the glory of God. Man is still rebelling against his Creator. Opportunity after opportunity, grace upon grace, man continues to deny God's sovereign rule on earth. Satan continues to use the same old tricks by saying, "If you eat this fruit, *you will be like God.*" What fruit, you may ask? The fruit of our wisdom, our choices, our ways; sex, drugs, pornography, premarital sex, abortion, divorce; the list is endless. What fruit has Satan being tempting you with? When will we stop trying to make up all the rules by trying to play God? When will we stop eating Satan's fruit of fame, popularity, status, sex, fame, and wealth? When will we finally give God all the glory? When we fail to do so, that is the bad news.

The Foundation

"God is Love"

What was the ultimate reason for Jesus Christ to come to earth to live a perfect life for us, to die for all our sins, and to resurrect again in power? We touched on God's purpose to declare His glory to all creation. There is another reason. It is simply because He is God. To find this next reason, we must trace the question back to something in the character of God himself seen in His love and justice. God is love, and His love requires perfect justice. The love of God is one of the causes of the Gospel of Jesus Christ. 1 John 4:8 states, "God is love."

If God is love, then love requires a person to love, and that person is then given a choice to love back or reject. Love requires a love relationship between the two. Technically, God could have just basked in the love of the Father, the Son, and the Holy Spirit. But in His great love for us, he created us in His image to either love Him or reject Him. In one of the most popular Bible passages, John 3:16 tells us that it is this same love with which God loved the world. To demonstrate the depths of His love for the world, He sent His one and only Son to live, die, and rise again for all who would believe and turn to Jesus.

The justice of God requires that the righteous and holy judge deal correctly with the penalty due to us for our sins. A holy God has to be separate from sin and cannot be in fellowship with anything that is not holy. Romans explains God sent Christ to bear God's wrath and be a "propitiation" for our sin (Rom. 3:25), meaning to appease God's wrath. Paul goes on to say it was *"to show God's righteousness* because, in his divine forbearance, he had passed over former sins" (Rom. 3:25). This explains how the saints in the Old Testament were saved. It has always been by faith in Jesus Christ. God held back His wrath towards those in the Old Testament until the atonement of the sins of the world was paid for by Jesus Christ: "It was to prove at the present time that He himself is righteous and that He justifies him who has faith in Jesus" (Rom. 3:26).

Therefore, God's love also requires perfect justice upon both the Jew and the Greek. There is no distinction with God; all fall short of the glory of God (Rom. 3:22-23; Rom. 10:12-13). God is *love,* and God is *just*; these two character attributes of God were the reason God sent His one and only Son to love and justify us. We love God because He first loved us (1 Jn. 4:19). Yet while we were still sinners, God revealed His love toward us by sending us the one He values more than His own life, His one and only Son (Rom. 5:8). God did not wait around to love or save us for doing something good or by waiting for us to straighten our lives out. He loved us even when we didn't deserve love. That is a gracious and loving God!

Moses, Paul, and Jesus himself demonstrate the love of God. They all had the heart to separate themselves from God for the sake of others, a different kind of identity. Moses was willing to have his name blotted out of God's book of life for the sake of Israel. Paul was willing to give up Christ for the sake of his fellow Jewish brothers. Christ left heaven and gave up everything for you and for me. The heart of a true follower of Jesus is willing to sacrifice everything for someone else. That is *agape* love. I didn't understand true sacrifice until I had my first-born baby. As I read the Bible to my newborn baby, I read the words of Jesus from John 15:12-17 (NET):

> *My commandment is this—to love one another just as I have loved you. No one has greater love than this—that one lays down his life for his friends. You are my friends if you do what I command you. I no longer call you slaves, because the slave does not understand what his master is doing. But I have called you friends, because I have revealed to you everything I heard from my Father. You did not choose me, but I chose you and appointed you to go and bear fruit, fruit that remains, so that whatever you ask the Father in my name he will give you. This I command you—to love one another.*

Jesus was asked in Matthew 22 what was the most important Law. Jesus replied that the greatest thing we can do is love God and love people. This is the Great Commandment. Jesus went on to say that loving people and God fulfills the entire doctrines of the Bible. I thought I knew what love was until my wife and I had a miracle baby. All the doctors and professionals said it was impossible for us to have children. But there she was at home in her crib for the first time. I thought to myself there is nothing impossible with God. Then I asked God if it was wrong for me to give up everything for my little girl, even at the expense of separating myself from God. He answered that if I was willing to lay down everything for another, I would be doing exactly what He had commanded me to do. Giving my life for others was the start of knowing God's will for my life. What God was beginning to teach me that night would change everything. Loving God and loving people are the foundation.

I began to understand that God's one and only Son separated himself from God's presence by leaving heaven for the sake of all those who would believe in Him. He was even willing to be forsaken by His Father on the cross. Jesus has given us a perfect example of love. Just as I was willing to go to hell to fight for my little girl, if somehow she wasn't saved, Jesus was willing to go down to the darkest parts of the earth and fight for all mankind. As I stared at little Trinity in her crib, the Father was also staring down at His one and only Son as He came to us in the manger. As I contemplated God's will for my little girl, God the Father had already conceived before the foundation of the world His will for His one and only Son, who would suffer and die a horrific death for all mankind.

Don't miss this incredible example of love from the Father and the Son. Jesus lived a perfect life for us; He died and suffered excruciating pain on the cross to forgive us of all our sins, and on the third day, He showed us what it is like to live in resurrection power. Jesus gave all He had to demonstrate His love for us all. But don't miss this. The fruit doesn't fall too far from the tree of His Father. The Father allowed the one thing He valued more than His own life to live, suffer and die, and rise again on the third day. This is a different kind of love. As a father, I would die for a lot of people. But if I had the power, I would not ever allow any harm or pain to happen to my child. I don't know of any father who would do this, except One.

I began to look at my baby girl, and I still could not fathom letting her suffer and die for anyone but God, who, in His Fatherly love for His creation, so loved the world that He sent His one and only Son, that whoever would believe in Him would not perish but have everlasting life. In God's wisdom, He knew that through the sacrificial death of His one and only Son, millions of sons and daughters would come to Him to the praise of His glory. I began to understand, in a deeper way, God's divine love and knowledge that surpasses all human understanding.

I knew this was the truth that no other so-called religion could touch. The Father loved His creation so much that He sent us His one and only Son. I get tears just trying to write that fact. The Father sent us something that He values more than His own life. This is love. This is also the only thing that is going to change hearts because it is the undeniable truth of God. God is love. God's love is what compelled Him to send us His Son. How can anyone ask, "Does God love me?" Just remember Jesus' arms open wide on the cross; that is how much He loves you.

Again, I heard that quiet voice within me ask, "Do you trust Me?" As I continued to contemplate what God was telling me, I realized He knows a lot better than I do. If God wanted to take Trinity from me to save thousands of people, then His will be done. I finally came to the point of answering that quiet voice within me that was asking, "Do you trust Me?" My reply was, "Yes, I trust you, God; your will be done." At that moment, I began to see a glimpse of God's love in my own life. How amazing it is to know He truly has the whole world, including a little tiny baby, in His hands.

As I woke up the next morning, my whole outlook on life had changed. I never looked at people the same way again. Instead, I saw little newborn babies, God's little love miracles. I reflected on the day Trinity was born, remembered how I fell in love, and immediately knew this love was unconditional. I held her in my arms with a father's embrace. Now I can see my little girl in others and, with that, an incredible love for you, the reader. The deceptions of this life have made us something God never intended us to be. God loves you.

I saw a drug dealer on the corner, deceived by physical abuse, which led him astray. I saw a homeless woman, deceived by sexual abuse at an early age, causing her to give up on life. I saw a teenager who was suicidal because his father had beaten him. In response, he turned to the deception of gangs. I saw a prostitute who had turned to the deceptions of the streets and drugs because her father had sexually abused her. I could go on and on about those I have seen deceived by a worldly identity instead of turning to God.

You may be asking how I knew about these people. I saw my little girl in them, and that love motivated me to become part of their lives. The Gospel not only saved me, but it also empowered me to go share it with others so they may be set free. I approached them and asked if they knew how much God loves them. There is nothing I wouldn't do for my little girl, so there was nothing I wouldn't do for them. Not only did I see Trinity in them, I saw Christ in them. Matthew 25:40 says, "Truly I say to you, to the extent that you did it to one of these brothers of mine, even the least of them, you did it to me." Sharing Christ is the greatest gift of love I could ever give to anyone. As long as I live, I will fight for my little girl and for every person God loves. Sacrificial love is at the core of being a true disciple, a true follower of Jesus Christ. And as we become followers of Jesus, He teaches us the importance of sacrifice, as the apostle Paul states in Romans 12:1-2 (NET):

> *"Therefore I exhort you, brothers and sisters, by the mercies of God, to present your bodies as a sacrifice—alive, holy, and pleasing to God—which is your reasonable service. Do not be conformed to this present world, but be transformed by the renewing of your mind, so that you may test and approve what is the will of God—what is good and well-pleasing and perfect."*

The world has deceived us and conformed us to live an identity based in its ways and its standards. Paul tells us we must ReAwaken, renew our minds to understand God's will for our lives. It starts with trusting God and His ways, not the world's ways. It starts with loving God and loving people, which is revealed by our sacrifice for them, as Jesus commanded us in John 15:12-17.

The fact is, the darkness in this world has caused an *Identity Crisis* within all our souls. Perhaps you have suffered disappointments, pain, unwise relationships, sickness and disease, homelessness, loneliness, betrayals, or financial concerns, or perhaps you've just been stagnant. Maybe you have sought direction to understand the point of life, only to discover that every step is without aim. As a result, your life seems to be in a crisis. With all the confusion, maybe you're asking such questions as: "Who am I? Why am I here? What is my purpose? How can God love me?"

I have Good News for you! When you are willing to ReAwaken to God's purpose for your life by seeking His identity, your entire life will change. Even though we see and experience the darkness that creates crises in our world every day, a spiritual light shines in that darkness, a light that can lead us to a new life, a new identity of power; a ReAwakening. We have an opportunity to be transferred from the kingdom of darkness to the kingdom of light. Our past can be changed, and our future bright because of our new powerful identity.

The world will never stop throwing deceptions our way, but there is Good News. There is a divine, unconditional love for every soul of man and

The Foundation

woman in this life from a Heavenly Father who will free us from our *Identity Crisis* and lead us on the journey to experiencing a personal relationship with Jesus Christ.

God has written eternity on all the hearts of men and women, and that is worth giving our lives for. We were created in the image of an incredible Heavenly Father who gave us something worth living for and dying for. And when you find the One worth dying for, you ReAwaken in power. I pray that this book will be a step in your pursuit of ReAwakening the powerful identity that God created for you.

ReAwakening power, joy, purpose, and meaning in this life means stepping toward the one who revealed our original intended identity to the world. This book is a pursuit of truth that reveals the transforming power of God to make us new. I pray you would have the courage to seek out eternal life! I write this book because of God's unconditional love for us all. It changed my life, and it can change yours too. May the kingdom of God, His power, and His glory suddenly come upon all who read of His great love for us all!

What is the Good News?

The phrase "Good News" comes from the Greek word "euangelion," which means the Good News of Jesus Christ. The Greek word "euangelizo" means to proclaim the Good News. Other words used for the Good News could be *the atonement, justification,* and *salvation.* The atonement is the central doctrine of the Good News and is seen in the most popular passage in the Bible:

> *"For God so loved the world that*
> *he gave His only Son, that whoever*
> *believes in Him should not perish*
> *but have eternal life" (Jn. 3:16).*

The bad news was birthed when our identity was put in a crisis by our first parents' sin (Rom. 5:12). When Adam and Eve turned to Satan's ways, we all entered into an *Identity Crisis.* Some may ask why is there so much pain, so much evil, so much injustice, so much hate, and no more healthy values. The Bible tells us once we turned from God, He gave us over to the consequences of that poor choice (Psalm 81:11-12). All the bad and evil in

What is the Good News? 57

this world is due to our turning our backs on God. Funny how we want to blame God for everything. This is what created our *Identity Crisis*. We are in crisis because we were created in the image of God (Gen 1:26-27) to be holy like God is holy (1 Pet. 1:16). Our spiritual reality is dead because of our sin. God created us to be like Him so that we could love Him and our neighbors as ourselves. When we sin, we are sinning against God's created design. Satan continues to say, "Did God really say?" When Satan tempted our first parents, he created a God-shaped hole in all of us. That God-shaped hole in our hearts could never be filled with anything in Satan's world. That God-shaped hole can only be filled with Jesus Christ. If we continue to sin and seek the things of this world, we will experience constant guilt and regret. We go through our lives feeling that sense of dread, always feeling like something is missing. The crisis is an echo of the pain of our hearts that longs to be filled with the relationship we were created to have with God.

I started this book by presenting our crisis in all its miserable detail, the bad news. Paul in Romans now proclaims Good News that allows sinners to be in the presence of a holy God, "But now a righteousness from God, apart from the law, has been made known" (Rom. 3:21). The declaration "but now" starts a new beginning for humanity. People can now obtain the perfect righteousness that is needed for heaven. Before the "but now," all stood condemned because of their sin. God's Law was given to show us that we could never be perfect and righteous by obeying the Law perfectly. The Law was given to show us we need a Savior. The Savior came to live out the Law and prophets perfectly for those who would put their faith in His righteousness (Matt. 5:17). Now God has provided a righteousness apart from the Law or human works. A righteousness that is given because of our faith in the righteousness of Jesus Christ. The Father loved His creation so much He sent us His Son to provide a way for us to be declared righteous. There is Good News of great joy for all the people. We can be saved through the life, death, and resurrection of Jesus Christ. We can move from crisis to Christ.

The Good News is that what we can't fix, an all-powerful God can fix. What is impossible with man became possible with God when He sent us His one and only Son (Luke 18:27). This is the ultimate act of love. Once God, in His love, decided before the foundations of the world to save human beings by the life, death, and resurrection of Jesus Christ, Scripture reveals that there was no other way under heaven in which man can be saved (Acts 4:12). Through Jesus, God rescued us from our sin and provided salvation. This is called the "Gospel of grace." Grace means a "free gift"—something we don't deserve or cannot pay for. Salvation is a gift from God from start to finish. Nothing we do could merit or deserve such an indescribable gift (Eph. 2:8-9). The Good News (Gospel) applies to all who believe in and receive Jesus Christ (Jn. 1:12). Our works do not earn God's grace; if that were the case, we could earn our salvation. We could take the credit. But the Bible is clear: Jesus saves. Our faith does not earn God's love or merit His grace.

The Garden of Gethsemane is a beautiful depiction of the absolute necessity of Jesus Christ.

What is the Good News?

There is no other way we can be saved but by Jesus Christ (Acts 4:12). Jesus prays, *"If it be possible* let this cup pass from me; nevertheless, not as I will, but as you will" (Matt. 26:39). Jesus reveals His humanity in not wanting to drink the cup of suffering. Jesus also reveals His deity in wanting to do the perfect will of His Father. This prayer indicates that if there were another way possible for people to be saved than through the suffering and death of Jesus Christ, it would have been done. This shows us the incredible love the Savior has for us, along with the Father. Amid the worst possible suffering and death imaginable, Jesus was willing to endure it because it was the only way. This reveals His great love for us all.

Jesus also confirms that He is the only way for salvation after His resurrection. Along the road to Emmaus, He has a theological talk about how to be saved with two of His disciples. The disciples were in crisis after they put Jesus to death, and Jesus responds, "O foolish men, and slow of heart to believe all that the prophets have spoken! Was it not *necessary* that the Christ should suffer these things and enter into His glory?" (Lk. 24:25–26). Jesus explains to the two disciples that this was the Father's plan prepared before the foundation of the world. As we look to the Old Testament, we begin to find many prophecies spoken about the necessity of the Christ suffering for the sins of the world.

Many people and many religions say there are many ways to heaven. The Bible emphatically teaches in over a hundred passages that Jesus alone is the way, the truth, and the life, and no one goes to heaven apart from Him (Jn. 14:6). This makes perfect sense. If the Father, who is all-powerful and all-mighty, could have stopped His one and only Son from suffering, He surely would have stopped it. If Jesus Christ prayed for this to be taken away, if it were possible, God would have heard His prayer and taken it away. There was no other way for the Father to save us than to send His Son Jesus Christ to live a perfect life for us, die on a cross, and forgive us all our sins, and to rise again on the third day to assure the same Spirit that raised Jesus Christ will raise us to new life now and in the future.

What Must I do to be Saved?

I believe this is the most important question on this side of eternity. This exact question was asked in Acts 16:30-31: "Then he brought them out and asked, 'Sirs, what must I do to be saved?' They replied, 'Believe in the Lord Jesus and you will be saved, you and your household.'" The Apostle Paul simply says, "Believe." He does not ask them to repent because the fact that they are asking how to be saved from sin is an act of repentance. In other words, "I get that sin kills, and I am willing to turn to Jesus Christ and do whatever I need to be saved from my sin." Paul did not ask about all the correct theology and doctrines. Turn to the Lord Jesus Christ to save you and believe in the Lord Jesus to save you.

What are we turning from? This can become a loaded question. In the general sense, we are to turn from trying to save ourselves with the things of this world. In the Garden of Eden, the narrative

What is the Good News?

explains what we are to turn from in Genesis 3:1–5:

> *Now the serpent was more crafty than any beast of the field which the Lord God had made. And he said to the woman, "Indeed, has God said, 'You shall not eat from any tree of the garden'?" The woman said to the serpent, "From the fruit of the trees of the garden we may eat; but from the fruit of the tree which is in the middle of the garden, God has said, 'You shall not eat from it or touch it, or you will die.'" The serpent said to the woman, "You surely will not die! For God knows that in the day you eat from it your eyes will be opened, and you will be like God, knowing good and evil.*

Satan tempts Adam and Eve to turn to something that is not of God. Eat the fruit, and God knows you will be like Him. He then gets bold and says, "Did God really say the day you eat you will die? You surely won't die." Satan doesn't want us to trust God's word, so he changes and perverts the very word of God. So no longer do they trust in God, but they turn to something else.

Adam and Eve are the mother and father of the human race. Because of their one act of disobedience, all were credited with sin. This is called "Total Depravity." When we turn to something other than God, which is sin, sin enters the world and affects the whole human race. Romans 5:12: "Therefore, just as through one man, sin entered into the world, and death through sin, and so death spread to all men because all sinned." The Bible says sin produces death and eternal separation from God. We now must be saved from sin that produces death. The Bible says Satan is a liar and deceiver. When Satan said, "you surely won't die," this was the greatest lie. Sin produced death in all humanity. We turned to sin to save us, which produced death, and now we must turn back to God to save us.

What is the minimum we must do to be saved? This has become one of the most difficult questions for me as an evangelist to answer. There are many reasons. First, addressing and understanding the sovereignty of God. God has elected us to be saved before the foundation of the world (Eph. 1:4). So being saved is more about our awareness of being saved before the foundation of the world. Our names were written by the author in the Lamb's book of life before the foundation of the world (Rev. 13:8). God is the author and perfecter of our faith (Heb. 12:2). God is the one who began the work, and He is the one who will be faithful to complete it (Phil. 1:6). With that in view, we must look at the criminal on the cross with Jesus in answering what is the minimum we must do to be saved. Jesus' words during the crucifixion reveal the minimum or the start of what we need to know to be saved. The events of the cross reveal the minimum for salvation. Luke 23:32–43:

> *Two others also, who were criminals, were being led away to be put to death with Him. When they came to the place called The Skull, there they crucified Him and the criminals, one on the right and the other on the left. But Jesus was saying, "Father, forgive them; for they do not know what they are doing." And they cast lots, dividing up*

What is the Good News?

His garments among themselves. And the people stood by, looking on. And even the rulers were sneering at Him, saying, "He saved others; let Him save Himself if this is the Christ of God, His Chosen One." The soldiers also mocked Him, coming up to Him, offering Him sour wine, and saying, "If You are the King of the Jews, save Yourself!" Now there was also an inscription above Him, "THIS IS THE KING OF THE JEWS." One of the criminals who were hanged there was hurling abuse at Him, saying, "Are You not the Christ? Save Yourself and us!" But the other answered, and rebuking him said, "Do you not even fear God, since you are under the same sentence of condemnation? And we indeed are suffering justly, for we are receiving what we deserve for our deeds; but this man has done nothing wrong." And he was saying, "Jesus, remember me when You come in Your kingdom!" And He said to him, "Truly I say to you, today you shall be with Me in Paradise."

Jesus was murdered by the people of the world, but it was still God's sovereign plan for the Son to suffer for the sins of the world. God's sovereignty must never be taken lightly. As the all-powerful Jesus Christ was crucified, He could have wiped out the world with two words: "Be gone." Instead of demonstrating His omnipotent power, He revealed His love with the words "Forgive them Father for they know not what they do." Jesus is the visible image of the invisible God (Col. 1:15). The Father knew Jesus would reveal true love. We know love by this: He laid down His life for us (1 Jn. 3:16).

Jesus came as the Savior of the world and freely chose to give His life over for the ransom of many. Jesus' dying for the sins of the world reveals the height and depth of God's love for us all. The Father always knew this in His sovereignty. The Father also knew if this kind of love didn't change a person, nothing will.

At the end of Jesus' life, we see Him with the worst of sinners, two criminals. One of the criminals denies Jesus, the other acknowledges Jesus as a righteous man. One of the criminals admits his sin, acknowledges Jesus' majesty, and turns to Jesus to be saved.

This is the best illustration in the Bible about the minimum we must do to be saved by simply believing in the real Jesus Christ and turning to Him to save us. Maybe instead of saying the minimum, the beginning of what we need for salvation would be better. All the criminal on the cross did was see a righteous man who didn't deserve the crucifixion. He also believed this righteous man could save him when he said, "Jesus, remember me when you enter your kingdom." Jesus said, "Today, you will be with me in paradise." This is an indication that the criminal was saved. What did he do to be saved? I see only two things. First, he saw and believed in Jesus as a righteous man who didn't deserve to die. Second, he believed Jesus could save him from his confessed sin.

What does this show us? First, the criminal believed in the real Jesus Christ. It was the real Jesus Christ that saves us. Today, there are many forms of Jesus Christ in other religions that are not the real Jesus Christ. Also, today we cannot experience

What is the Good News?

the incarnational Jesus Christ. This shows us that we must first **believe** in the real Jesus Christ presented in the word of God, the Bible. Second, we must recognize our sinful state that leads to death and simply **turn (repent)** to Jesus Christ to save us from our hopeless predicament.

Let's explore this further by asking a few questions. Did the criminal on the cross understand soteriology? Did he understand the nature of the atonement? Did he understand justification? Did he understand Calvinism or Arminianism? Did he understand the concepts surrounding God's sovereignty and freewill of man? Did he understand the substitutionary atonement? Did he understand the penal substitution? Did he understand any correct theology or doctrines? Let me sound blasphemous for a moment. Did he understand that Jesus was God? The answer has to be no.

Watch closely; how could anyone in that day understand or believe that an all-powerful God, an almighty God, could be crucified and put to death by the people He created? It was impossible for the culture of the time to believe that an omnipotent God could die. If the disciples and Apostles abandoned Him in the confusion of an all-powerful God allowing His creation to crucify Him, what chance did the criminal have in believing Jesus was God? I am not saying to deny the deity of Christ. Jesus Christ is the Great I am, and only God can forgive sin. If Jesus wasn't God, then we are still in our sins. What I am saying is this is what is needed to begin the process of salvation.

What did the criminal believe? He believed in the real righteous Jesus Christ, and then he turned to

Jesus to save him. Paul says to believe in the Lord Jesus Christ, and you will be saved. Most people at this point will not be aware of all the theological doctrines surrounding the atonement, nor will they understand the deity of Jesus Christ. One important disclaimer. I believe in the sovereignty of God surrounding our knowledge of the Gospel. I believe nothing can happen apart from God allowing it. Jesus says, "No power can be given unless it been given from above." (Jn. 19:11). This doesn't mean He created evil, but He allows evil and turns it around to reveal His purposes and glory.

I believe that He who began the good work will be faithful to complete it (Phil. 1:6). I believe that everyone who believes in the real Jesus Christ of the Bible and turns to Jesus to save them from their sin will be saved by God's sovereign hand upon the process of salvation. Saving faith will increase our knowledge and understanding of all the aspects of the Gospel. The more we learn about the Gospel, the more we trust in the Gospel, the more we begin to reveal the power of the Gospel.But the start of knowledge always has a beginning. We may or may not come to a complete knowledge of the Gospel. Our coattails may be on fire when we enter heaven (1 Cor. 3:15). Yet the more we know, the more we live out the power of the Gospel in the present. I will share the complete Gospel as we go further into the book.

A Closer Look

What is needed for salvation? As mentioned above, knowledge has a beginning. Believing in the real Jesus of the Bible and turning to Him to save us from our sins is the beginning. The major fact we must understand to be saved is that we are sinners, and we need to trust Jesus Christ to save us from our sins. This is the minimum or just the beginning. Again, we must understand that God's sovereignty oversees the entire process of salvation. God will give us the knowledge we need to fulfill His calling. I don't want to touch on every aspect of salvation but would like you to beware of what is called "The Order of Salvation" as presented in Wayne Grudem's *Systematic Theology:*

"The Order of Salvation"
1. Election (God's choice of people to be saved)
2. The Gospel call (proclaiming the message of the Gospel)
3. Regeneration (being born again)
4. Conversion (faith and repentance)
5. Justification (right legal standing)

6. Adoption (membership in God's family)
7. Sanctification (right conduct of life)
8. Perseverance (remaining a Christian)
9. Death (going to be with the Lord)
10. Glorification (receiving a resurrection body) [6]

It starts with Election, the Effectual Call (the Gospel Call goes to everyone; the Effectual Call goes to those who respond by faith); Regeneration; and then Conversion. Conversion is where we begin to play a role by faith in the life of the Lord Jesus Christ. Just as a newborn baby doesn't have a part in its birth, so is it with a born-again Christian. For example, it is not the faith of the baby that allows the baby to create its birth, it is the parents that start the process. It is the same with our spiritual Father God, who starts the process in the first three components of salvation.

First, let's look at faith. A good definition of biblical faith is trusting the Lord Jesus Christ to save us from sin, which produces death. Faith (Greek "pistis") is the noun for what we believe in. Believing (Greek "pisteuó") is the verb and is our action as we grow in our faith. We put our faith in the life, death, and resurrection of Jesus Christ. As we come to know Jesus Christ more, we begin to put our faith into action, which is living out His life, death, and resurrection.

Adam and Eve turned to Satan and trusted his advice to be saved by eating the fruit of this world. Satan also tempted Jesus to worship him and said he would give Him all the kingdoms of this world if He would just bow down to him. Jesus worshiped and turned to His Father alone. We now must have faith in Jesus Christ that encompasses trust in Christ alone to save us from our sins. Entering heaven requires perfect righteousness that every human being falls short of. Romans tells us that now a righteousness apart from the Law (human effort) has been revealed (Rom. 3:21). God's requirements for heaven is holy perfection. Romans 3:23 tells us that no human being can meet that requirement; we all fall short of the glory of God. Nothing we do in our human effort can ever obtain the perfect righteousness of God. But now, there is Good News of great joy for all the people. "But now," a righteousness from heaven has been revealed by faith alone in the perfect life Jesus Christ lived on our behalf. God credits that perfect righteousness to our account when we trust in Him. Jesus' life is what fulfills the perfect requirements for heaven.

The second is true repentance (turning; a change of mind) from our sinful ways and trusting Jesus to forgive us and save us from the consequences of all our sins. The word "metanoeo" is a verb meaning *to repent*. The word "metanoia" is a noun meaning *repentance*. In its basic form, it means "to change our mind" or "to turn." Here is where the confusion begins among Christian theologians about what the word *repent* means. I would almost consider myself a reformed theologian, but I can't, due to three main explanations of repentance, election, and reprobation. I don't place myself in any specific theological camp because, in one area or another, I disagree.

The importance of defining repentance is crucial. I believe faith and repentance are needed for salvation. But how we define repentance changes everything. If we look within the biblical context, it seems to make perfect sense. In the four Gospels, the world had just denied and crucified the Savior of the world as a criminal, a blasphemer. They decided that obedience to the Law is all they needed for salvation. In other words, they did not need a Savior to save them; they believed they could follow the Laws and obtain their own righteousness. Now in the book of Acts, they must change their minds about achieving their own righteousness by acknowledging their sin and change their verdict about Jesus Christ. They must turn from viewing Him as a crucified criminal and turn to believing in Him as the Savior of the world. They must turn from trying to save themselves (one mistake disqualifies us from obtaining His perfect righteousness and heaven) and turn to the Savior to save us.

Satan has deceived us to think that eating the fruit of this world can satisfy and save us. Once we realize it can't, we need somewhere else to turn. Dr. Phil and Oprah Winfrey were not available to those in biblical times. Neither were all the books on self-help that say they can save you from just about anything. All these false systems of the world cannot fill that God-shaped hole in our hearts that only Jesus can fill. Only Jesus can save. It might be a rough road for a lot of people in coming to an awareness that nothing in this world can save them. Suffering the things of this world can be difficult. Nevertheless, at some

A Closer Look

point, people will come to the end of the road of this world. The Bible says there is now Good News of great joy for all the people who turn from the ways of the world and turn to Jesus Christ to save them.

I lean toward reformed theology except on a few key points as mentioned above. Repentance is one of them. They use phrases like *forsake your sin, turn from your sin, surrender to the Lordship of Jesus Christ* as defining the repentance needed to be saved. They may also say those that don't believe in their definition of repentance don't believe that Jesus Christ being Lord is needed for salvation. That is false. What I do (surrender) doesn't depict whether Jesus Christ is Lord. He is Lord of my life and Lord of all. What He has done for me depicts Jesus as Lord. He has conquered all my sins and credited me with His perfect, righteous life. My question is simple. Do I have to forsake all my sin? Do I have to turn from all my sin? Do I have to surrender all to be saved? No matter how hard I try, I can't seem to forsake my sins. I want to stop, but I can't. I want to turn from all my sins, but I can't. I want to surrender all to Jesus, but I can't. What a wretched man that I am. Who will save me from this body condemnation? Paul says it best in Romans 7:24–8:4:

> *Wretched man that I am! Who will set me free from the body of this death? Thanks be to God through Jesus Christ our Lord! So then, on the one hand I myself with my mind am serving the law of God, but on the other, with my flesh the law of sin. Therefore, there is now no condemnation*

> *for those who are in Christ Jesus. For the law of the Spirit of life in Christ Jesus has set you free from the law of sin and of death. For what the Law could not do, weak as it was through the flesh, God did: sending His own Son in the likeness of sinful flesh and as an offering for sin, He condemned sin in the flesh, so that the requirement of the Law might be fulfilled in us, who do not walk according to the flesh but according to the Spirit.*

Let me say it this way. I can't turn, forsake, and surrender correctly. I tried as a single pastor for over ten years and could not defeat pornography. I did everything in my strength to turn, forsake, and surrender it to God. I knew Jesus was Lord of all and received Him as such. I loved Him as much as a person could. I would have died for Him in a blink of an eye. I battled day in and out hating my sin. Paul tells us we can't turn from our sin because nothing good dwells in us, for the willing is present in me, but the doing of good is not (Rom. 7:18).

Then, I decided I am going to turn to Jesus Christ and trust Him alone. I am going to change my mind about the power of the Gospel. It is not about what I do but what He has done. When the Father sees you, He sees what Jesus has done. It has all been paid for. I found victory. I found power. I found sin had finally lost its hold on me. Jesus paid the penalty for my present sins, my past sins, and my future sins. Sin no longer had power because Jesus had removed it as far as the east is from the west. I found sin was an illusion that Sa-

A Closer Look

tan, the deceiver, wanted me to believe still held power. I found the power of the Gospel. I turned to Jesus' perfect life of forsaking all, surrendering all, turning from all on my behalf. I fully accepted His free indescribable gift of righteousness. I realized I would rather stand before a holy God depending on what Jesus did in forsaking sin, turning from sin, and surrendering all. Not what I do, but what He has done. The next thing I realized, by the love and grace of God, I began to walk like Jesus. I began to walk in the power of the Gospel. When sin truly lost its power over my life, it also lost its hold on me.

Let me clarify it one more way. Let's say I am an alcoholic. I receive, believe, and turn to Jesus Christ to save me. I can't just turn from the alcoholic addiction cold turkey. I turned to Jesus, but I still battle the alcohol abuse because it numbs the pain, the hurts, the anxiety, the fear, the worry. As I begin knowing more about Jesus, I start going to Him more and more. Turning to alcohol less and less and I begin to turn to Jesus more. The key thought here is that I first turned and believed in Jesus to save me. When I do that, I am credited with His righteousness, not my own. Even though I am trying to turn from my sins, I can trust Jesus who turned from sin perfectly for me. The more I began to understand the power of the Gospel, the more sin loses its power and grip over me. I begin to realize that alcohol is just a Band-Aid; Jesus Christ's victory in life, death, and resurrection is the cure. Christ's life, death, and resurrection is my salvation.

The third is hope in the resurrection of Jesus

Christ. Hope may be defined as a future faith. As I die to sin, the power of the resurrection becomes my hope. I hope to live like Jesus in my own resurrection. As I hope for the resurrection, I find it in power. The New Testament goes on to expand our hope in the resurrection of Jesus Christ. Peter states, "we have been born anew to a living hope through the resurrection of Jesus Christ from the dead" (1 Pet. 1:3). Peter is directly tying the resurrection of Jesus Christ to the Gospel. Jesus's life, death, and resurrection were examples for us to follow to a new life of power. This resurrection life has a now and not yet fulfillment for us. Jesus says, "The glory which You have given Me I have given to them, that they may be one, just as We are one" (Jn. 17:22).

A Christian is a disciple and is to reflect the glory of God given to us by Christ to the world. Jesus also says, "Go into Jerusalem and wait until you receive power to be my witnesses" (Acts 1:8). Jesus is saying go wait until you receive power. This power is the resurrected Christ in us by the power of the Holy Spirit. The word for witness in the Greek is "martyr." In other words, go into Jerusalem and die to yourself, and you will be filled with the power of the resurrection. There can be no resurrection without death. It is the Holy Spirit that raises us in resurrection power. Remember, holy means separate from sin. Ephesians 4:30 and First Thessalonians 5:19 commands us to not quench the Holy Spirit with our sin. Sin is the Christian's kryptonite. Finally, Paul tells us that it is Christ in us that is the hope of glory for the world (Col. 2:27).

Jesus not only credits us with His perfect life, but He also credits us with His resurrected life that is just like His. Again, this is the *now not yet* concept, and we do not receive the fullness of that new "resurrection life" now, for our bodies continue to rage war against sin and are subject to weakness. But in our weaknesses, the Spirit of God is strong with new resurrection power.

It is the example of His resurrection that Christ credits us with a new kind of life when we put our hope in the resurrection. Paul says God "made us alive together with Christ (by grace you have been saved) and *raised us up with him*" (Eph. 2:5-6; cf. Col. 3:1). When the Father saw Christ raised from the dead by the power of the Holy Spirit, He also saw us being raised "with Christ." The words *raised* and *seated* are in past tense. It is already a done deal to God. If this amazing identity and inheritance is our reality, why don't we feel blessed and privileged to walk in it? Remember we are credited with the life, death, and resurrection of Jesus Christ. Just receive it by faith as a free gift. The Gospel of Jesus Christ not only saves us but it is an example for us to live out our new power-filled lives. Paul states, "that I may know Him and the power of His resurrection ..." (Phil. 3:10). It is Christ alone and the power of the Holy Spirit that Reawakens the Gospel in our lives so we can live the way God created us to live—in His holy image.

My second book, *Identity Crisis*, focused on helping us move toward a Kingdom Empowered Identity. This identity is beyond anything we could ever think or imagine. Our identity is empowered by the Holy Spirit and resurrection power. Paul's focus for the Ephesus church was that they would experience and know this power; "What is the immeasurable greatness of his power in us who believe, according to the working of his great might which he accomplished in Christ when he raised him from the dead and made him sit at his right hand in the heavenly places" (Eph. 1:19–20).

The Bible is teaching us that the same resurrection power that raised Jesus Christ from the dead is the same resurrection power that is working in us. This new life is a process that reflects the Gospel of Jesus Christ's life, His death that suffers and crucifies our sins until we are dead to sin, and resurrection that occurs when we die to sin than we can rise to a new resurrected life. There has to be a death before there can be a resurrection. Paul states the process; "We were buried therefore with him by baptism into death, so that as Christ was raised from the dead by the glory of the Father, we too might walk in newness of life ... So you also must consider yourselves dead to sin and alive to God in Christ Jesus" (Rom. 6:4, 11). Our new life represents a new identity away from our worldly identity crisis to a new identity in Christ.

The new identity and resurrection power provides everything we need to live a new life in Christ Jesus and to live in God's original image that He created us to live in (2 Pet. 1:3; Rom. 6:14; cf. 1 Cor. 15:17). Jesus talks about this power that will be ours to reflect Christ to the world (Acts 1:8). We are, therefore, to be witnesses of the resurrected Christ as the resurrected Christ lives again through our lives. Jesus Christ in us is the

A Closer Look

hope of glory for the world (Col. 1:27). That is why Jesus tells us, "Take My yoke upon you and learn from Me, for I am gentle and humble in heart, and you will find rest for your souls. For My yoke is easy and My burden is light" (Matt. 11:29-30). Our strength and power come from the resurrected Christ, who lives in us. We are dependent on Christ's strength, not ours. This makes ministries' yoke easy and the burden of ministry light. A huge danger is that we become very legalistic in what we do and depend on man instead of depending on God, who lives within us. The reason so many people criticize the church today is because they do not see the resurrected Christ in the church. What they are seeing is man-made laws, traditions, and regulations that quench the resurrection power. We are more concerned with paying the pastors salary, paying the church building mortgage, paying for the one hundred-thousand-dollar cost on audio equipment, and other concerns. Notice this was never a concern of the early church.

The early church's new resurrection power for proclaiming the Gospel was spreading throughout the world with the working of miracles, signs, and wonders. The reason for this power was there were no hindrances as there are today. The early church died so it could live. The early church overcame their Roman enemies even when they faced death. Overcoming their opposition was given to the disciples after Christ's resurrection from the dead, and their new resurrection-powered identity characterized their lives. They lived without fear of death because their faith was in the resurrection. What was the worst thing that could happen to them? They die and go be with the Lord, and that is a bad thing?

Ever since the Roman emperor Constantine married Rome to the church, we have begun to slowly lose our resurrection power. It was no longer about Jesus alone. It became about big church buildings, fame, and popularity of the popes, a monopoly on biblical doctrine, money and wealth and power. Take, for example, the Roman Catholic Church's rise to power. The church so lost its way it beheaded people, burned people at the stake, sold indulgences so people could buy their way into heaven, all in the name of Jesus Christ. What is our faith in today as a church? Great music and entertainment, big buildings, nice chairs, top of the line audio equipment, the most famous pastors and teachers. Oh, how the mighty have fallen.

Our new identity in Christ makes us one with Christ. Our union with Christ includes all three components of the Gospel of Jesus' life, death, and resurrection. In our current resurrection power, we can partake in the glory of God in part (Jn. 17:22-23) as we reflect the resurrected Christ to the world. Later, we will receive our resurrected bodies that will sin no more, and we will finally be in the complete image God originally created us to be. But until then, we still live with the not yet glory of the Lord and in His resurrection power to proclaim the majesties of Him who called you out of the darkness and brought us into his marvelous light (1 Pet. 2:9). Don't miss what Paul is saying in Ephesians 2:4-6:

A Closer Look

But God, being rich in mercy, because of
His great love with which He loved us, even
when we were dead in our transgressions,
made us alive together with Christ (by
grace you have been saved), and raised
us up with Him, and seated us with Him
in the heavenly places in Christ Jesus,
so that in the ages to come He might
show the surpassing riches of His grace
in kindness toward us in Christ Jesus.

This text may be the most profound in Scripture. While we were enemies of God, the Father did something that no one could ever fathom. The best way to get to know someone would be if that person could somehow live through your life. The Father made us one with Jesus Christ so we could know Him by watching Him work His resurrection power through our lives. The word grace is rendered as a free gift. This gift is too amazing; there could be no amount we could pay to receive such a gift. How could you possibly do anything to merit the God of all creation graciously loving you so much that He would live through your life? This gift is priceless.

Paul goes on to confirm his point. The words "saved," "raised," and "seated" are past tense, meaning this is already a present reality. You see, we are the body of Christ. We reign with Jesus, are seated with Him, and raised with Him as He reigns from heaven. As Jesus reigns from heaven on His throne, we are an extension of His body, His hands, His feet, His words; we are in Christ and Christ is in us. Why does God do this? Again, back to Acts 1:8, to show the world through our lives the proof of the resurrected Christ as He lives again in you and me.

The only way Christians and the church are going to spread the Good News of Jesus Christ across our land is if they become resurrected Christians living in resurrection power. We already talked about this process, but for the sake of its importance, let me explain it again. We are not only saved by the Gospel of Jesus' life, death, and resurrection, but we also live in the life, death, and resurrection of Jesus Christ. When we believe in Jesus, we begin to reflect His life; when we reflect His life, suffering and persecution comes as we die to our sins; and when we die to our sins, we can finally experience a resurrection. We share in the authority of Christ as it is in heaven. Jesus says in the Great Commission that all authority was given to Him; now He has given it to us to go share the Gospel and make disciples of all nations. As we fulfill the Great Commission, we know He will never leave us or forsake us because He is within us (Matt. 28:16-20).

This is the most incredible message on this side of eternity. It can present itself as three triple sided coins.

The first coin represents **faith, repentance,** and **hope**. All three work together. As we have more faith in the Lord Jesus, we surrender and die more to the sins in our life; and then we hope more for Jesus' life to be reflected through our life by resurrection power.

The second coin is the Gospel of His **life, death, and resurrection**. Our faith is in the righteous life of Jesus, our repentance in His death as we die to our sin (Rom. 6), and our hope is in the resurrected Christ living in us in power.

The third coin manifests Christ's **righteousness, freedom,** and **power**. Our faith is in the life of Jesus, which credits in us His righteousness; our repentance joins us to His death that frees us from sin, and our hope is in the resurrection which reveals power in our lives. The table below lays this out for us.

PROCESS	REAWAKENING GROWTH PROCESS		
Salvation	FAITH= *Pistis*; noun; our faith The more we believe, the more we reflect His life	REPENTANCE= *Mentanoia*; noun; what we believe. The more we repent, the more we die to sin	HOPE The more we hope, the more we reflect His resurrection
Sanctification	LIFE Believe = *Pisteuó* The more we believe in His life, the more we grow in the likeness of His life. The more we reflect His life, the more righteousness we become	DEATH Repent=*Metanoeo* is the verb. The more we repent, the more we die to sin. The more we die, the more freedom we obtain	RESURRECTION The continued hoping of the resurrection allows us to be partakers of the resurrection. The more we resurrect, the more power we have
Glorification The *now not yet* concept	RIGHTEOUSNESS This is the end result	FREEDOM This is the end result	POWER This is the end result

The Complete Gospel

The complete Gospel is what a disciple of Jesus Christ should present to nonbelievers. I always preach the life, the death, and the resurrection of Jesus Christ. I would rather be safe than sorry. When it comes to the most important message on this side of eternity, I want to make sure I miss nothing. In this section, we consider the main aspects of Christ's work in the Gospel: (1) Christ's LIFE of obedience for us, in which He obeyed the requirements of the Law in our place and was perfectly obedient to the will of God the Father as our representative; (2) Christ's DEATH for us, in which He took the penalty for all our sins and as a result, died for all our sins to propitiate and take the Father's wrath; (3) Christ's RESURRECTION for us, in which He rose again on the third day to a new life to ensure us that we also will ReAwaken to a new resurrected eternal life in the future and in the present. Our purpose is to walk in our new resurrection-empowered life to do the will of the Father.

It is important to notice that the emphasis and the primary influence of Christ's work of redemption are rooted in God the Father. Who loved us so much, He sent the one thing He values more than His own life, His one and only Son? Jesus obeyed the Father in our place and perfectly met the demands of the Law. And He suffered and died in our place, receiving in himself the penalty of God's wrath that God the Father would have visited upon us. Jesus then rose again with a ReAwakened life that demonstrates how we are to walk in new resurrection power. In all three cases, the Gospel is always the primary way in which the Father works. God the Father and God the Son secured our salvation by the power of the Holy Spirit.

One question I always ask people I share the Gospel with is, "What would you do if your one and only child gave their life for someone, and they never told anyone about what your child did for them?" I would be a little angry. Let's look at the flip side of that question. What would you do if your child gave their life for someone and all that person did was talk about what your child did? I don't know about you, but if someone always told others about my child, I would bless them. Listen to what Paul says in 2 Timothy 4:5, "But you, be sober in all things, endure hardship, do the work of an evangelist, fulfill your ministry." In this text, doing the work "of an evangelist" is a prepositional phrase. We know that Timothy was a gifted pastor in Ephesus and not necessarily an evangelist. Timothy was to do the work of an evangelist. Paul was the actual evangelist. Paul is saying that if you do the work of an evangelist and share the Gospel, you will fulfill your pastoral ministry in Ephesus. Why is this? Think about it. What do you think the

Father in heaven is going to do when you tell the world what His one and only Son did for them? He is going to bless your socks off.

Some Christians say they are not evangelists, so they don't have to share the Gospel. I tell them there is a Greek word for that kind of thinking: "baloney." All Christians are called to share the Gospel of Jesus' life, death, and resurrection. Some may say, "I don't know how." Same Greek word: "baloney." If you are saved by the Gospel, then you know how to share the Gospel. This is the one thing I know we are supposed to do on this side of eternity. No more excuses!

Jesus' Life

Jesus Christ is the name above all names. A lot is revealed in the name Jesus Christ and how He is the perfect author and finisher of our faith. The name Jesus means "deliverer," and He was sent to set us free from the power of sin. Christ simply means "anointed one." God the Father anointed Jesus before the foundation of the world to be the Savior of the world. God spoke through His prophets in the Old Testament about the coming of the promised deliverer who would come with an anointing from above to save His people from their sin (Acts 3:18–20). Jesus came as God the Son and was the exact representation of His Father (Col. 1:15). The amazing aspect of Jesus is that He was fully God and fully human at the same time (Gal. 4:4–5; Phil. 2:6–11). He came into the world to become like us in His incarnation (incarnate means "in the flesh") so that we could relate to God. Every aspect of Jesus' life was in humility. He was born of a virgin; He was birthed in a manger with animals; He had no place to lay His head. Christ was not of this world. This is why it is so important to die to the things of this world so that we can experience an unhindered resurrection of our own. If the world has no power over us, we stop seeking the things below and freely start seeking the things above. A ReAwakening will occur. Jesus has given us an example to follow by becoming human. He has shown us the process of how to honor, glorify, and be obedient children of God. Christ's holiness demonstrates the image God originally intended for us to live in. A life full of love and emptied of the world and selfishness would be willing to love others like Jesus (1 Jn. 3:16). Through Jesus "Exampleship" (the title of my next book), we learn how to live in our new identity in Jesus Christ, to be created in the image God.

Christ came to live in perfect obedience to God. The theological term is called His "Active Obedience." Christ did not only die for our sins, but He had to become righteousness for us. If Christ had only died for the forgiveness of sins, He could have died at a much earlier age. He tells John the Baptist in Matthew 3:15, "It is fitting for us to fulfill all righteousness." Jesus had to live His life fully so that He could fulfill all righteousness for us by fulfilling all the Law and prophets for us perfectly (Matt. 5:17). Both perfect righteousness and forgiveness of our sins are what is needed for heaven. If Jesus dying on the cross was the only thing needed for heaven, then we would find ourselves in the exact same position as Adam and Eve before they had sinned. God allowed them to be tested to verify their ability to be righteous. They failed and confirmed that only God is righteous. To live in paradise (The Garden of Eden) forever with God, they had to prove that they could be righteous by obeying God forever. If they could have been righteous, then Jesus would not have had to obtain righteousness for them. Paul clearly says, "God made him who had no sin to be sin for us so that in him we might become the righteousness of God" (2 Cor. 5:21).

Salvation completely involves the three components of Jesus' life, death, and resurrection. His life credits us with righteousness; His death forgives us of our sins and sets us free from the power of sin; His resurrection assures us our hope and power in this life. Being declared righteous in the presence of a holy God requires Christ's righteousness to be imputed to us, for our sins to be imputed to Christ, and for the power of Christ to be imputed in us. Then the Father no longer sees what we do but what Christ has done. We are declared justified and righteous in the presence of a holy God because of Jesus' life, death, and resurrection.

Christ had to live a life of perfect righteousness to God in order to earn righteousness for us. He had to obey the Law and prophets fully for His whole life on our behalf so that we would be imputed, or credited, with His perfect obedience. Again, it is called His "Active Obedience;" the flip side of this is His suffering and dying for our sins, which is called His "Passive Obedience." Both His Active and Passive Obedience are needed for heaven. Again, not just the forgiveness of sins but the imputation of perfect righteousness. Paul reveals in Romans

His "Active Obedience," now a righteousness apart from the law has been revealed. If only the hearers of this message could have understood the depths of this good news. Paul says it is no longer what we do but our faith in what Jesus Christ has done, "*not having a righteousness of [his] own* based on law, but *that which is through faith in Christ* the righteousness from God that depends on faith" (Phil. 3:9). Paul says that Christ alone has been made "*our righteousness*" (1 Cor. 1:30). Paul continues to say, "For as by one man's disobedience many were made sinners, so by one man's obedience many will be *made righteous*" (Rom. 5:19). This is amazing Good News; amazing grace has now been revealed from heaven.

One of my biggest pet peeves as an evangelist is when evangelists do not proclaim the necessity of Jesus Christ achieving a lifelong record of perfect righteousness for us. They simply proclaim that Christ had to die for our sins and thereby pay the penalty for our sins. But such a position does not adequately explain why Christ did more than just die for us; He also became our "righteousness" before God. Jesus said to John the Baptist before He was baptized by him, "It is fitting for us *to fulfill all righteousness*" (Matt. 3:15).

The word for crediting us with His perfect life is "imputed" righteousness. Imputation or justifying righteousness restores the righteousness that humanity lost through Adam and Eve's original sin (Rom. 5:18-19). God has mercifully dealt with our sin by imputing our sin on the person of the crucified Christ. The Father is also able to judge us according to His mercy as being declared to be righteous in Christ. God accomplished this saving work through the cross in order "to demonstrate His justice at the present time, so as to be just and the one who justifies those who have faith in Jesus" (Rom. 3:26).

The question we should ask ourselves is whose lifelong record of righteousness would you rather depend on when you're standing before the holy Judge of all creation, Christ's or yours? Think of it like this. You have two options. First choice: record your life on a video from birth to death and hand it over to a holy God. You both will look at the video together, and one mistake condemns you forever. Remember, He is a holy and righteous God. Or you can choose the second option. Jesus Christ records His life from birth to death and allows you to substitute your bad film for His perfect film. If you accept His gift, He will give His film to the Father so He will judge you according to what Christ did. Christ will nail your old film to the cross with himself and bury it forever.

The film Christ gives to His Father will depict His entire life on earth, from the time of His birth to the time of His death and ascension into heaven. As God reveals the film of Christ's life, He sees us as being "in Christ." That is, whatever Christ did on earth, we did with Him. Everything Christ did, we have been credited with as we were in Christ. We are not actually in Christ until we receive Jesus Christ. Jesus then has His Father review the video of His perfect life on our behalf. As the Father watches that video, He sees us with and in Christ.

The good thing about this beautiful doctrine called the "substitutionary atonement" is God saw us as being "in" Christ; the bad is He also saw our sins as belonging to Christ. God made Him who knew no sin to become sin on our behalf (2 Cor. 5:21), and "the Lord has laid on him the iniquity of us all" (Isa. 53:6). Christ did not die for His sins, but our sins were in Christ and He died for our sins. "He himself bore our sins in his body on the tree" (1 Pet. 2:24; Rom. 4:25; 1 Cor. 15:3; Col. 2:14; Heb. 9:28).

God not only saw our sins in Christ, He saw us in Christ. When Christ lived, when Christ died, when Christ resurrected, God saw us as being with and in Christ. Our old identity was *"crucified with him"* (Rom. 6:6). Paul states, "I have been crucified with Christ" (Gal. 2:20). He also tells the Corinthians that "One has died for all; therefore all have died" (2 Cor. 5:14; Rom. 6:4–5, 8; 7:4; Col. 1:22; 2:12, 20; 3:3; 2 Tim. 2:11).

This is one amazing identity. God saw us as living with Christ, having been dead and *buried* with Christ, resurrected and *raised* with Him, and *taken up to heaven* and seated with Him in the heavenlies. Paul makes this clear, "And raised us up with Him, and seated us with Him in the heavenly *places* in Christ Jesus" (Eph. 2:6; see also Rom. 6:4–11; 1 Cor. 15:22; Col. 2:12–13). Therefore, when Christ returned to heaven, all the blessings of salvation were earned for us through His life, death, and resurrection. God saw all of this as ours because we were in Christ, and now Christ is in us. We have been blessed with every spiritual blessing in the heavenlies in Christ (Eph. 1:3). In the Greek, *every* means every. God gave us these blessings because He saw us in Christ as if we had earned them ourselves. We are united with Christ. We are one with Christ. One of the things that actually drives me as an evangelist is that if I can present these truths accurately, who, in their right mind, would not receive Jesus Christ? The inheritance that is ours in Christ is the greatest message on this side of eternity. This gives me some comfort for those who reject the Good News. I could mourn their rejection but realize God is the one who sovereignly Reawakens this truth in people. The reality is that there must be really something missing in someone who rejects Jesus Christ and the Gospel.

Jesus' Death

We see the amazing love of both God the Father and God the Son in redemption. Not only did Jesus know that He would bear the incredible suffering of the cross, but God the Father also knew that He would have to inflict this pain on His own deeply loved Son. "God shows his love for us in that while we were yet sinners Christ died for us" (Rom. 5:8).

Christ's Sufferings for us is theologically called His "Passive Obedience." Not only did Jesus obtain righteousness for us in His "Active Obedience," He also suffered and died for the sins of the world in His "Passive Obedience." His life credits us with His "Active Obedience"; His death credits us with His "Passive Obedience" that pays the penalty for all our sins.

Christ left the kingdom of God and the presence of His Father because of His love for us. In doing this, Christ entered into a satanic kingdom that would cause the Savior much suffering throughout His entire life. Even at His birth, His parents endured many hardships. This is what happens when the light begins to shine in the darkness of Satan's world. Jesus was the light of the world and suffered for most of His life in the darkness of Satan's world. Christ's sufferings would eventually lead to an excruciating death on a cross; His whole life in Satan's fallen world involved suffering. The suffering at the cross was so horrible they had to make a new word for that kind of suffering: "excruciating," which means "out of the cross."

The Gospels reveal a life of suffering; Jesus suffered during the temptation in the wilderness without food or water (Matt. 4:1–11). On top of that, He was tempted and attacked forty days by Satan. As the Son of God, He learned obedience through suffering; "Although He was a Son, He learned obedience from the things which He suffered" (Heb 5:8). His entire life was filled with persecutions, hate towards Him, and tremendous suffering. He faced tremendous opposition and attacks from His own people throughout the majority of His ministry (Jn. 1:11; Heb. 12:3–4). The prophet Isaiah mentions the outcome of the "Suffering Servant" predicting the coming of the Messiah; "He was despised and forsaken of men, A man of sorrows and acquainted with grief; And like one from whom men hide their face He was despised, and we did not esteem Him. a *man of sorrows* and acquainted with grief" (Isa. 53:3).

The more Jesus Christ was reflecting the light to the world throughout His ministry, the more his sufferings intensified as He drew near to the ultimate suffering. The Bible seems to be silent about Jesus' life before the start of his public ministry, but after He began his ministry is when all hell broke loose on the Savior of the world. He said to his disciples, "My soul is deeply grieved, to the point of death; remain here and keep watch with Me" (Matt. 26:38). It was the excruciating suffering of the cross that Hell attacked the most; the enemy went on an all-out assault to stop the Savior for taking away the sins of the world. Satan initially may have thought he won the victory; that was until the third day. Satan must have then realized you can't keep the only good man down. Even death couldn't defeat our mighty Savior.

The New Testament makes it clear that our Savior's death was all-sufficient. His ultimate sacrifice paid for all the sins of the world once for all time (Heb. 7:27). For the Christian, this is amazing Good News. Sin no longer has power over your life. Jesus paid the penalty for your past sins, your present sins, and even your future sins. The only power sin has is when the father of lies, Satan, deceives you into thinking that sin still has power to corrupt your life. Don't believe the lies. He wants to cause as much crisis as he can so you never look to Christ. Glorify the Son by believing in the power of the Gospel. Walk in the freedom and victory Christ has provided you. It is an awesome identity.

The blood of Christ is confirmation that His life was put to a sacrificial death to pay the penalty for all our sins. The blood of Christ represents His death and its sufficiency to forgive and remove all our sins. Not only does it forgive us all of our sins, but it also removes all the guilt associated with sin. The Bible teaches that the blood of Christ cleanses our consciences (Heb. 9:14), gains us bold access to God in worship and prayer (Heb. 10:19), constantly cleanses us from remaining sin (1 Jn 1:7; Rev. 1:5b), is able to help us conquer the accuser of the brethren (Rev. 12:10–11), and rescues us out of a sinful way of life (1 Pet. 1:18–19).

Christ's death is theologically called the theory of "*Penal Substitution.*" Christ's death was "penal" in that He took the penalty for our sins. Christ's death was also a "substitution" in that He took our sinful lives and nailed them to the cross and substituted His eternal and sinless life for ours. No amount of doing good before a holy God could ever pay the penalty for sin, nor could it satisfy the wrath of God. I began the book by asking, "What are you willing to die for?" When you understand the truth of this incredibly Good News that gives you an incredible new identity and inheritance, the answer becomes easy. Jesus Christ! The apostle Paul says, "I have been crucified with Christ and it is no longer live I who live but Christ Jesus lives in me" (Gal. 2:20).

If you want your life to make an impact on this side of eternity, there is no other way to do so that extends beyond the grave. It is no longer about what we do; rather, it is all about what Jesus Christ has done. We live, we serve, and we will stand before a holy God because of the life, death, and resurrection of Christ alone. There is no other way. Our spiritual position—our incredible identity—is unified in His. It may sound foolish to die for something on this side of eternity, but when we are willing by faith to put our trust in the Lord Jesus Christ by dying to self, we will experience a new identity filled with resurrection power. The only thing we may say when we finally experience our new resurrection life is, why did we wait so long to trust the Lord Jesus Christ with our life?

The secret to this resurrection power is again rooted in believing the life of Jesus, trusting the Lord to die to your sins, and in death of sin experiencing the power of the resurrection. If this incredibly Good News is true, it means all our sins are already nailed to the cross. We just have to believe it. We will never be sinless on this side of eternity, but we can by faith walk in the power of the one who became sinless for us. All the Christians' kryptonite has been nailed on the cross. Anything that could separate us from the love of God is gone (Rom. 8:38). Paul says, "nothing can separate us from the love of God" (Rom. 8:39). In the Greek, *nothing* means nothing; our sins, our guilt, our mistakes, and everything else (Rom. 8).

When we begin to realize that God sees us as He sees Jesus, it begins to free us from our past fears and hurts, and we begin to walk in the righteous justification that is ours in Christ. Justification is not simply a doctrine developed in the heat of the battle of our *Identity Crisis*. The more we see ourselves clothed in the righteousness of Christ, the more we begin to walk in our ReAwakened Identity.

Several key truths must be understood as we begin to understand how Christ has justified us. The concept of justification surrounds our legal standing before God. Through the work of Jesus Christ on the cross, Jesus has legally declared us justified in God's eyes by removing the penalty for our sins. Romans 3:23 says that sin produces death, and without sin, there is no death. Jesus was without sin and yet died. Jesus died for our sins and for our imperfections. Jesus died in my place and in your place. It should have been me on that cross and you on that cross, but it was our righteous King who died in our place. In dying in our place for our sins, He removed the power of sin in our lives completely by forgiving us of our past sins, our present sins, and even our future sins.

As a result, we no longer have to feel the sin-producing guilt that Satan uses to make us feel guilty and unworthy. Instead, we experience the life-giving Spirit, who produces conviction of our sin. This conviction reveals to our spirit that we are no longer slaves of sin in the kingdom of Satan, but citizens of righteousness in the kingdom of God. 1 John 4:13 teaches us that conviction produces for us the awareness to repent and confess our sins so we can continue to experience our new identity. Where there is no holiness, there is no power. Where there is sin, which is Christians' kryptonite, there is no Gospel power.

The Son of God had no sin and was a sort of Superman for our world. But even Superman could not compare to our all-powerful, loving Savior. The Son chose on His own free will to suffer and die on a cross and accepted the penalty of death. He also took on God's wrath that we deserved. Since the Son of God had no sin, His willingness to suffer on a cross and accept the penalty we deserve is far beyond what any fictional character called Superman could provide. Christ's great work wipes out anything we could ever do. That is why Paul says, "When we are faithless, he remains faithful because he cannot deny himself" (2 Tim. 2:13). Jesus imputed His life to us, to deny us is to deny himself. The Father accepted Jesus' life as a substitute for our punishment (1 Pet. 2:24). He paid the price for our sins to a holy Judge that we could never pay (Psalm 47:7–9; Tit. 2:11–14). His life declares us righteous; His death sets us free from our sins; and His resurrection unites us to Him in power. That is Good News.

Justification also reveals what we call the "Substitutionary Atonement." Jesus's work at the cross reveals that He substituted His perfect life for your imperfect life. He nailed your sinful and imperfect life to the cross and credits you with His eternal, perfect life in return. When we receive the King into our hearts as our personal Lord and Savior, Christ's righteousness is imputed to us. The Father no longer condemns us for what we have done, what we are doing, or what we will do. Instead, He sees what Christ has done, what Christ is doing, and what Christ will do through us.

Our justification is a one-time event when God declares an eternal decision to give us eternal life. John 10:28 teaches that nobody can take our eternal position from us because it was issued by the hand of God. It is God's promise and a free gift to us, and from Scriptures such as Romans 11:29, we know the promises of God are irrevocable. If we could lose our justification, we would have never really received eternal life. Instead, we would have only received temporal life. Our justification removes any legal recourse or accusation against us. Paul mentions this in Romans 8:33-34: "Who shall bring any charge against God's elect? God is the One who justifies." Yet Satan continues to defy God's sovereign decision by continually asking, in deception, "Did God really say?"

I have Good News for you: God really did say that we are justified through Christ Jesus, our Lord. "The Greatest Story Ever Told" is not fiction. Even if God's amazing grace may seem too amazing for us to grasp, it still remains our reality. Our identity before God has been forever and eternally changed. When God sees us, He sees the King. If that is the case, then we have been given a new power-filled identity to go and be witnesses of the power of the King and His kingdom as He lives again, in us and through us.

There are no words to express what Jesus did for us. The gift is indescribable (2 Cor. 9:15). It should have been me on that cross, it should have been you on that cross, but it was the Savior of the world. This idea is often called the theory of "*Vicarious Atonement.*" A "vicar" is someone who takes the place of another as a representative. Christ's life, death, and resurrection was, therefore, "vicarious" because He lived in our place; He died in our place, and He rose again in our place as our example and representative. What an indescribable Savior.

Jesus' Resurrection

Not only are we united to the life and death of Christ, but we are also united to the resurrection of Christ. Paul writes, "I have been crucified with Christ and I no longer live, but Christ lives in me" (Gal. 2:20). Those words have been my refuge as a Christian for the past thirty years. Any time I prepare to preach, teach, or proclaim the Gospel, I always say those words of Paul. It is not me that is at work, but it is Christ who is in me. Go to work, Lord Jesus, and do what only you can do through me by the power of the Holy Spirit. These words assure us of this new identity that is ours in Jesus Christ, this incredible resurrection power.

Not many evangelists share the third part as being part of the Gospel. I believe this to be a great error. Because of all that Jesus Christ has done for us we ought to offer our lives back to God as living sacrifices (Rom. 12:1). A sacrifice is dead and can only come back to life again with resurrection power. This is a key aspect of the Gospel we rarely mention. The moment Adam ate the fruit that God forbid them to eat, they surely died. It seems the text has a conundrum, but the death they died was a spiritual death on that day (Gen. 2:17). The consequence of that sin would also produce a physical death many years later.

Adam's sin was in direct disobedience to a command of God. God gave them only one command and the human heart couldn't obey. This was a probational period for Adam and Eve to see if they could obey God perfectly and obtain righteousness. The original parents of humanity failed horribly and brought humanity under sin's death penalty (Rom. 5:12). This is often called "Total Depravity." Just like Adam and Eve, we are spiritually dead in our sins and transgressions (Eph. 2:1). Spiritually dead people can't make themselves come back to life again; it takes resurrection power to bring someone to life again. This is called "Regeneration" in the "Order of Salvation." When God raised Jesus from the dead, He broke the curse of sin's power of death (Rom. 5:17). What the one man did by bringing sin and death to all humanity, God responded in mercy and grace by sending us His one and only Son to live a perfect life, die on the cross, and resurrect by the power of the Holy Spirit to cancel out the effects of the original sin (Rom. 8:11; 1 Cor. 15:15–20). Jesus' life, death, and resurrection prove that God's substituted our sinful lives for Jesus' perfect eternal life.

Because of the good news of Jesus Christ, our lives have been changed and created for eternity. In the wisdom of God, the church now reflects the resurrected Christ through millions who are part of the body of Christ. Christ died but now the church becomes witnesses of the resurrected Christ to all the world (Acts 1:8). This incredible mystery gives us the full insurance of our inheritance in Christ and that we are blessed with every spiritual blessing in the heavenlies in Christ (Eph. 1:3). This union with Christ is the incredible mystery that Paul talks about in the book of Ephesians. Even though we experience the now power of the resurrection in our mortal bodies, our mortal bodies will someday die and be reunited with Christ to await our new sinless resurrected bodies. Our new identity in Christ is something too amazing to be made up by any man. All that was Christ's is ours and all we are is Christ's. We all belong to Christ, our new master who purchased us with a high price (1 Cor. 7:23).

Paul rejoices over this new identity that is ours in Christ through His life, death, and resurrection. The life, death, and resurrection not only saves us, but by the power of the Holy Spirit, the Gospel of Jesus' life, death, and resurrection are reflected in our lives when we believe and surrender to Jesus Christ. The ways of the world start to grow greatly dim in the light of knowing and serving Christ. Our wants and desires start to become kingdom-focused instead of worldly focused. The more we die to the world, the more we live with a kingdom mindset. We are called to die with Christ, and in doing this, we die to the influences of the world (Rom. 7:6; Gal. 2:20; 5:24; 6:14; Col. 2:20). The more we die to the things of this world the more we experience the power of His resurrection. There can be no resurrection without dying with Christ as Paul states: "Therefore we have been buried with Him through baptism into death, so that as Christ was raised from the dead through the glory of the Father, so we too might walk in newness of life" (Rom. 6:4). Paul continues, "Even so consider yourselves to be dead to sin, but alive to God in Christ Jesus" (Rom. 6:11; 1 Pet. 1:3; 2:24). Our new identity in Christ gives us everything we need to live a godly life in Christ Jesus (2 Pet. 1:3); our new identity is "made complete" in Christ (Col. 2:10–13); we have become a "new creature" in Him (2 Cor. 5:17); and our new identity is not rooted in the crises of this world, but in Christ in heaven (Col. 3:1–3).

The resurrection of Jesus Christ is what brings us to a new life and a new identity. Peter tells us, "Blessed be the God and Father of our Lord Jesus Christ, who according to His great mercy has caused us to be born again to a living hope through the resurrection of Jesus Christ from the dead" (1 Pet. 1:3). Here the importance of the resurrection being part of the Gospel is verified. Peter connects the resurrection with salvation and our new birth in Christ. Jesus' resurrection is an example of the new life we can have. The resurrection is our hope and insurance that the same Holy Spirit that raised Jesus from the dead is the same Holy Spirit empowering us in this life (Rom. 8:11). Jesus lived a new life for us, and now it frees us to live just like Him. We have already obtained the perfection of Christ that frees us to press on toward the upward call of Jesus Christ to obtain that which He has already obtained for us (Phil. 3:14-17).

It is by the power of the resurrected Christ working in us by the power of the Holy Spirit that we enter into this indescribable identity. Our identity resides in everything that Christ is and everything that Christ has done. This is the secret of the Christian faith, having faith alone in what Christ has done alone. Our victory and power are not dependent on what we do, our mistakes, our failures, our sins, but on having faith in the power of the Gospel and what Christ has done. When God raised Jesus from the dead, our identity was in Christ. God saw us as having the same power being raised "with Christ" and Christ's resurrection. Paul knew and lived the power of the Gospel when he says, "That I may know him and the power of His resurrection ..." (Phil. 3:10). Paul knew that this life was all about reflecting the resurrected Christ in our new identity by receiving power to be His witnesses to the world. Paul emphasizes our incredible new identity in Christ when he says in Ephesians 1:19-20:

> *What is the surpassing greatness of His power toward us who believe? These are in accordance with the working of the strength of His might which He brought about in Christ, when He raised Him from the dead and seated Him at His right hand in the heavenly places, far above all rule and authority and power and dominion, and every name that is named, not only in this age but also in the one to come.*

Paul's focus is reminding us that the same power that raised Jesus from the dead is the same power that lives in us. Paul teaches that all the aspects of the Gospel must also be lived out in our lives when he states in Romans 6:4-11:

> *Therefore we have been buried with Him through baptism into death, so that as Christ was raised from the dead through the glory of the Father, so we too might walk in newness of life. For if we have become united with Him in the likeness of His death, certainly we shall also be in the likeness of His resurrection, knowing this, that our old self was crucified with Him, in order that our body of sin might be done away with, so that we would no longer be slaves to sin; for he who has died is freed from sin. Now if we have died with Christ, we believe that we shall also live with Him, knowing that Christ, having been raised from the dead, is never to die again; death no longer is master over Him. For the death that He died, He died to sin once for all; but the life that He lives, He lives to God. Even so consider yourselves to be dead to sin, but alive to God in Christ Jesus.*

This new identity is focused on allowing the resurrection power to fill us as we grow and mature in our Christian lives. Again, the main barrier to this resurrection power is sin, the Christians' kryptonite. The more we die to sin (Rom. 6:2), the more sin loses its power in our lives, "For sin shall not be master over you" (Rom. 6:14), but Jesus becomes Lord; Lord means master. What is the master of your life, sin, or Jesus Christ? The reality in our world today is that sin has become our master. We are still eating the same fruit that Satan tempted Adam and Eve with; "Eat this fruit and you will become like God." The world wants to be its own god by making up its own rules. We become tolerant of everything and truth is subjective. The church was birthed in Acts 2 when one hundred and twenty believers were willing to die to their ways and trust the absolute truth of the word of God. Jesus is resurrected from the dead and Jesus is Lord and Savior of the world. Jesus told them to wait in Jerusalem until they receive this new identity of resurrection power. The power of the Holy Spirit fell upon the believers and they were given the same power that raised Jesus from the dead, to be witnesses of the resurrected Christ in them and to proclaim the Gospel. This same power is available today for those who are willing to receive the power from above by living out the Gospel by faith alone in Jesus' life, death, and resurrection.

Redemption

This final point may scare a lot of people. The reality is that we are still in bondage to our sins and the unseen demonic forces. The more you share the Gospel and minister to those in need, the more you will experience the reality of the darkness. When you start living as a light in the darkness is when all Hell breaks loose. Many Christians will never experience the reality of this darkness because they are not a threat to the kingdom of darkness. When you truly live "All for Jesus," that is when the dark forces attack. That is why Paul tells us to put on the full armor of God and get ready for battle (Eph. 6:10-18). Paul tells us our battle is not against people but against the darkness in Ephesians 6:11-12:

> *Put on the full armor of God, so that you will be able to stand firm against the schemes of the devil. For our struggle is not against flesh and blood, but against the rulers, against the powers, against the world forces of this darkness, against the spiritual forces of wickedness in the heavenly places.*

We need to be redeemed from sin and the forces of the Devil. Paul tells us in Galatians 5:1: "It was for freedom that Christ set us free; therefore keep standing firm and do not be subject again to a yoke of slavery." We live and dwell in the kingdom of darkness, and our old identity as a fallen people reflects our bondage to sin and to Satan. We need the Savior to constantly set us free and "redeem" us out of that bondage. If we don't constantly stand firm in Christ, we will lose many battles. Satan even tried to keep the Savior of the world in bondage by tempting Him with the same thing he tempted Adam and Eve with: "Did God really say (Matt. 4:1-11)?" The battle belongs to the Lord (2 Chron. 20:15). Satan is always trying to get us to deny the very word of God and worship him instead of our Creator.

As I spoke of earlier in the book, we are in Satan's domain of darkness when he was cast down to the earth from heaven. Lucifer was a reflector of God's glory in heaven throughout eternity, and then unrighteousness was found in him, and he was cast down to the earth and became Satan to play the leading villain in "The Greatest Story Ever Told." John tells those who are in Christ, "We know that we are of God, and that the whole world lies in *the power of* the evil one" (1 Jn. 5:19). Christ came to set us free from the power of the evil one, and if the Son sets you free, you are free indeed (Jn. 8:36). Christ came to defeat the darkness that has enslaved us "and might free those who through fear of death were subject to slavery all their lives" (Heb. 2:15). The beauty of the Gospel is that not only have we been set free from the dominion of darkness, but we have become partakers of the kingdom of God on earth as it is in heaven. "For He rescued us from the domain of darkness, and transferred us to the kingdom of His beloved Son" (Col. 1:13). We have received a new identity that has been set free from the dominion of sin (Rom. 6:11), and we are no longer slaves to sin but slaves to righteousness. "And having been freed from sin, you became slaves of righteousness" (Rom. 6:18). You have been saved to live out that which saved you, the Gospel. Through the Gospel of Jesus' life, death, and resurrection, we have a new identity:

> *"But you are a chosen race, a royal priesthood, a holy nation, a people for God's own possession, so that you may proclaim the excellencies of Him who has called you out of darkness into His marvelous light; for you once were not a people, but now you are the people of God; you had not received mercy, but now you have received mercy" (1 Pet. 2:9-10).*

We must take hold of our new identity and inheritance. We have one shot on this side of eternity to live out this new identity. Will we capture the moment?

What Now?

Ever since Satan deceived Adam and Eve, the whole world has encountered an incredible *Identity Crisis* and rebelled against its creator. As a result, rather than walking in its God-given identity, mankind is now walking in a world out of order, seen by the incredible sin and moral decay that surround society (Gen. 3-8:20) because Satan knocked God's divine order of creation out of balance. Unfortunately, sin will not leave sinful man alone, and it continues to separate God's people from His sovereign, intended identity. Yet mankind continues to live as though nothing has happened, refusing its desperate need for a new Kingdom Identity.

God has chosen you for a purpose; it's up to you to decide whether you want to follow all that God has planned for your life. The depths of this calling are far more than you can ever imagine or fathom. I heard an illustration that struck me: "The caterpillar is the most confused creature that roams the planet because undoubtedly stamped in his soul is the call to transformation." Caterpillars must go through stages before their metamorphosis is

What Now?

complete. They begin as eggs, hatch as caterpillars, and then go through a stage where they eat, and eat, and eat some more. Eventually, they become a chrysalis/cocoon before the transformation is complete, and they can finally emerge as beautiful butterflies.

Ecclesiastes 3:1 tells us, "To everything there is a season, a time for every purpose under heaven." Often, we want to walk straight into the calling God has for us. We want to do and be everything God wants us to be. We want to skip the journey that takes us there and do it *now*! We want to go from being caterpillar eggs to being beautiful butterflies! But we must remember the hardest times define us; the hardest times are when we learn and grow best. What doesn't kill us makes us stronger. We all know there are risks to anything being born prematurely. For anything to be birthed, whether it is a vision or a calling, to fulfill it, we must go through a process, a refining fire. We must go through stages and paths as preparation.

Sometimes our lives can reach a point where they seem routine and mundane. Like the caterpillars, we sluggishly move up and down, with no end in sight. We may feel bored with where we are. As we try to move across the road of life as a sluggish caterpillar, the cars that swarm down the road seem to promise an imminent threat. We begin to feel like God has forgotten us or as though we are not accomplishing much with our lives. The threat of crisis seems to come from everywhere. We go through the daily routine as a sluggish caterpillar with the danger of being hit by every crisis. Other times, we feel like we want to give up because we are waiting in a cocoon of despair that feels like death.

However, we should always remember that God, who began the work, will be faithful to complete it. He is working out everything for our good and is using every event to continue to transform us into a new eternal identity so we can accomplish the things God has stamped on our souls to do. We must continue to persevere and learn what God is molding us into during the valleys. After all, the clay doesn't say to the potter, "What are you molding me into?" Sometimes the molding hurts as God conforms us into the image of His Son. He uses hard times to mold us into something stronger.

Like the caterpillar, God wants to take us on a journey. There is a process, sometimes hard, sometimes grueling, sometimes painful. Job said, "For He knows the way that I take, and when He has tested me, I shall come forth as gold." Sometimes there is pain in the process. Sometimes the journey is difficult, but God knows and sees exactly where you are. When others see an ugly cocoon, He looks inside and sees the beautiful creature He is transforming into a butterfly.

God is planning and preparing our life and ministry to fly in His life, death, and resurrection like newborn butterflies. One late night, I was on my way home from church right after a member told my mother how bad a pastor I was because I didn't spend enough time with a member of the church's family. This particular member happened to be in turmoil and wanted the pastor to fix everything. We had over two hundred members at the time. I had spent many hours with the family, but

What Now?

no matter what I did, it wasn't enough. The pastor can't fix the problems but can only point you to the one who can. I prayed on the way home; the Lord spoke incredible wisdom into my life. He told me that He is the one who called me, not the members of the church. While God has called me to *His* purposes, a lot of the members of the church believe He called me to do and be everything according to *their* purposes. They believe I was called by them so I could fulfill their every need. I will never be able to meet that expectation, but I can point them to the one that already has met every need.

At that moment, I felt like a failure. As a pastor, I want to help everyone. In the continued silence of that prayer, the Lord asked me what I was trying to accomplish. I told Him I wanted to do as much as I could for Him before I stood before Him. I wanted to reach as many with the Gospel as I could, I wanted to travel the world sharing the Gospel, and I wanted to give my life for Him if He allowed me to. Then He said, "Why? I have already done that for you. No matter what you do, it will never be good enough, so I lived a perfect life for you. I saved the world for you. I lived a perfect life as a pastor for you. I lived a perfect life as a disciple for you. I loved for you, and I showed mercy for you. I even gave my life for all your mistakes. What exactly are you trying to accomplish that I haven't already accomplished for you?"

I was reminded once again of the foundation of our faith that we so easily take our eyes off when crises come. Jesus alone has credited us with everything: living a perfect life of perfect righteousness for us; dying on the cross to forgive us of all our sins and mistakes; rising again from the dead to give us the power to live like Him; teaching; leading; writing; loving; mercy; compassion; missions; evangelism; praying; discipling; pastoring—everything.

Let me give you an illustration. Let's assume you are running what is called the marathon of life that lasts a lifetime. There seems to be no finish line in sight with the threat of constant obstacles in your way as you run. Then Jesus steps in at the very beginning of the marathon and takes you all the way to the finish line and gives you His first-place blue ribbon. Jesus tells you I have won the race for you. Then He puts you back at the beginning of the race where He first found you. How do you run the marathon knowing you have already won? This should give believers incredible power and freedom to run the marathon of life. Knowing Jesus has already won the race for you is the great mystery of the church age. This Gospel foundation has always been taught since the beginning of my ministry, yet how easy it was for me to fall over the obstacles of crisis in the marathon of life and lose sight of the reality of the Gospel's power in my life.

As I pondered this indescribable gift, I began to cry. I was truly amazed at what Christ actually has done for us. He lived a perfect life for us; He died for all our sins, and He rose again for us in power. To ponder what this truly means is too overwhelming for a weak man like me to understand. I pulled my car over, totally overwhelmed by what Jesus has done for me. While being defeated by a church member, the Savior looked down at me with His eyes, clothed in His perfection, as if to say, "If they don't see you the way I see you, that is their problem." I realized that sick and sinful people hurt people. We must be stronger than those we serve. When we share the Gospel with those who are dead and buried in their sins, we must be a hundred times more powerful. Try to go share the Gospel at a cemetery sometime and see how many come back to life. Maybe a bad illustration, but if we don't have the resurrected Christ living in us, we are doomed to fail in bringing life to people through the proclamation of the Gospel. Be on guard; Satan uses immature people to devour and destroy His faithful servants. Be aware of his schemes and fight the good fight. Keep your eyes on Jesus and not the crisis. If we are looking at the crisis, our eyes are not on Jesus. How easy it has become to take our eyes off Jesus, the author and perfecter of our faith (Heb. 12:2). Turn from crisis to Christ.

In sharing the full Gospel of Jesus Christ, the church obeys Christ's purpose by living out the Great Commandment and obeys Christ's command for fulfilling the Great Commission. The church loves God the most by sharing what His Son has done. Afterward, the Spirit comes upon the church to complete His mission of making disciples. If your son or daughter gave his or her life for some cause, and then people went about fulfilling the cause without ever mentioning the reason why they can continue the cause—the sacrifice of your child—you would probably be pretty angry. In the same way, the church cannot be about the cause of Christ without first explaining the Good News about Jesus's life, death, and resurrection that allows the church to continue the cause.

The Gospel must be of first importance because it brings the power of salvation, from start to finish, to our churches. And rightly so! Can you imagine how pleasing it must be to the Father when we share what His one and only Son has done for us all? If we make sharing the Gospel our priority, the Father will open up the heavens and shower us with power and blessings. Wouldn't you, if someone talked about your child that way? Research states that less than 5 percent of Christians ever share Christ. Is that an obedient church? And we wonder why the church has lost its power. Let's make the Father rejoice as we share what His Son has done for us all.

The one thing the church must do is to be obedient to the commands of the Lord Jesus Christ. The one requirement that fulfills all the commands of Christ is sharing the Gospel of Jesus Christ. This demonstrates God's love fully. This was the focus of the early church in Acts and has been the focus of every spiritual revival that has taken place in the church since then. A church that has a burden for the lost and a passion for sharing the Gospel at any cost will become a resurrected church. Only then can the church reflect the glory of God before the Spirit of God can resurrect it to do its "greater works"!

Jesus lived through His life, was dead and buried, and rose again on the third day, as an example for us to follow. His life is a picture of the Spiritual Growth Stages I present in my book *Identity Crisis;* it provides a plan to follow to reflect His glory. The only way we can be filled with resurrection power is to first know Jesus and His life (see Phil. 3:10).

What Now?

As we grow in the knowledge and love of Jesus, we begin to live as 1 John 3:16 says: "We know love by this, that he laid down His life for us; and we ought to lay our lives for the brethren." In other words, when we see that Jesus laid down His life for us, we are moved to lay down our lives for Him. If by the Spirit, we lay down our lives, we will experience the manifestations of the power, comforts, and joys of our resurrection power (Rom. 8:13).

There comes a point when the church must realize everything Christ has done for her and forsake all for Him. The love of Christ is the church's motivation to move past the spiritual plateaus. The apostle Paul states it best in Romans 12:1-2:

> *"Therefore I urge you, brethren, by the mercies of God, to present your bodies a living and holy sacrifice, acceptable to God, which is your spiritual service of worship. And do not be conformed to this world, but be transformed by the renewing of your mind, so that you may prove what the will of God is, that which is good and acceptable and perfect."*

In other words, because of all that Christ has done for us, we should seek to be "All for Jesus!"

For all Christ has done for His bride, she must offer her life as a holy and living sacrifice to God. Paul uses a beautiful illustration of the Old Testament sacrificial system. An Israelite would present the best sacrifice possible, a sheep without blemish, at the temple. While these sacrifices would never be able to atone for sin (Heb. 10:4), they represented temporary forgiveness of sin that allowed the nation of Israel to worship in the man-made temple of God. God is holy and cannot be in the presence of sin, so there has to be atonement for sin.

According to 1 Corinthians 3:16, the church has become God's personally made temple of the Holy Spirit in which the power and presence of God dwells. Christ's work at the cross has removed the power of sin and paved the way for the Holy Spirit to resurrect the church. Jesus offered His life as a holy sacrifice to God to give the church an example to follow. When the church participates in the death of Christ, a resurrection is also expected, as Romans 6:4-5 indicates: "Therefore we have been buried with Him through baptism into death, so that as Christ was raised from the dead through the glory of the Father, so we too might walk in newness of life. For if we have become united with Him in the likeness of His death, certainly we shall also be in the likeness of His resurrection." Christ prepared the way for the church to live the Spirit-filled life. Christ has made the church a holy and consecrated temple ready for the indwelling Spirit; however, she still has a problem!

It is one thing to accept the gift of the cross of our Lord Jesus Christ by faith; it is an entirely different thing to live for Him by picking up our own crosses and living in resurrection power. Paul tells us in Romans 6:13 not to go on "presenting the members of our bodies to sin as instruments of unrighteousness; but present yourselves to God as those alive from the dead, and your members as instruments of righteousness to God." Christ has not only given the church eternal life, but He has also given her the incredible privilege to live as "a chosen race, a royal priesthood, a holy nation, a people for God's own possession, so that you may proclaim the excellencies of Him who has called you out of darkness into His marvelous light" (1 Pet. 2:9). God calls the church to power, but powerfully uses those who are willing to forsake all!

To build up the identity of the body of Christ, there has to be a body part willing to die for the head of the body. The church forsakes all for God, just like Jesus, and becomes resurrected to new life, just like Jesus. Before the church can hear the call, however, she must die. Can the church truly grasp the concept of death? I don't believe the church in the Western world truly does. Jesus says in Mark 8:34-37: "If anyone wishes to come after Me, he must deny himself, and take up his cross and follow Me. For whoever wishes to save his life will lose it, but whoever loses his life for My sake and the gospel's will save it. For what does it profit a man to gain the whole world, and forfeit his soul? For what will a man give in exchange for his soul?"

The church must die before it can truly live. Our society labels Christians as "hypocrites" because they live just like the world. Paul tells us to prove ourselves as those who are alive from the dead and do not continue to bring God dead sacrifices to God (Rom. 6). The church must depend on the power of God. If the church continues to live like the world by bringing God dead sacrifices, the world is never going to experience the resurrected church. I couldn't imagine what would have happened to Old Testament saints if they brought dead sacrifices to offer at the temple. That would be unheard of. They would always bring the best sacrifices.

When the church is willing to bring its best to Jesus, it will experience a Transformed Identity. The church will finally be prepared to be Jesus's witnesses by fulfilling its biblical mandate of fulfilling the Great Commission, but we must resurrect in power with the Holy Spirit (Acts 1:8). Israel missed their Messiah; has today's church missed the Holy Spirit? It is our tendency to go ahead of God, to not wait on the Holy Spirit. The church wants to be achievers instead of receivers. We want to save the world without the Spirit of God; however, the church's priority must be to pursue the power of the Holy Spirit at any cost. This is the age of the Holy Spirit, and we must let the Holy Spirit be the Holy Spirit.

In Matthew 28:16-20, Jesus commanded us to multiply through spiritual transformation. The Holy Spirit's mission is to provide the power for the church to fulfill the Trinity's mission. This is the focus of Missional Discipleship, which is the step of discipleship that reveals the power of the Holy Spirit in moving the disciple to action. To produce a correct action of the Holy Spirit requires transformation. Jesus's life, death, and resurrection provide a way for the church to participate in the New Covenant and reveal the power of God's kingdom on earth (Eph. 1:19-20). The only requirement for an individual to be part of this kingdom is to receive and believe in the King (Jn. 1:12). Jesus the King came preaching the Gospel of the kingdom, but when the people rejected the kingdom, they also rejected the King of that kingdom. So now the church must first preach the Gospel of the King, who people must first receive before they can experience His king-

What Now?

dom power on earth as it is in heaven. Before kingdoms can change, hearts must change.

For those of us who have already believed in the King, Jesus Christ has transformed our identity by making us citizens of His kingdom (2 Cor. 3:12-14, Phil. 3:20). The Good News is that God has sent His one and only Son to start the plan of redemption in us. Jesus's life, death, and resurrection provide the way for us to participate in this powerful movement of God's kingdom through the greatest healing and miracle of all—the forgiveness of our sins. Through the cross, God created a new people who can have a relationship with the living God, who are filled with the Holy Spirit, and who can walk in Christ's victory over the darkness.

Almost 2,000 years ago, Jesus left this world and wrote His final words with His blood on His hands: "My Father loves you. I love you. Give them the kingdom!" The Father established this plan before the foundation of the world that His glory may be established through His Son and His church. The Son not only reveals His love for us all, but He also reveals His Father's perfect mission and establishes a relational community built on the immeasurable love of His Father. Finally, the Holy Spirit has come to empower the church to fulfill Christ's mission by bringing God's kingdom on earth as it is in heaven. Will you surrender to the King and let the knowledge, the love, and the power of God's kingdom come upon you and create a new identity within you?

The Bible uses the expression "Union with Christ" or "in Christ" to express our indescribable identity with Christ. I call this our Kingdom Empowered Identity. It is beyond anything we could ever think or imagine. It encompasses the whole order of salvation. Ephesians 1:4 tells us that God elected us in Christ before the foundation of the world. And this ensures that He who began the good work of salvation will be faithful to complete it (Phil. 1:6). Jesus is the one orchestrating our salvation from start to finish; He is the author and perfecter of our faith (Heb. 12:2). This blessed hope and assurance should not produce complacency; on the contrary, it should compel us to surrender all to the sovereign King. Our Identity in Christ ensures us we have been blessed with every spiritual blessing in the heavenly places in Christ (Eph. 1:3). This ensures us all the benefits of salvation: our calling, regeneration, conversion, justification, adoption, sanctification, and glorification to the "praise of His glory" (Eph. 1:6; Rom. 8:29-30, 38-39; 1 Cor. 1:30; Jn. 15:1-11; 1 Jn. 2:5- 6). Our entire past, present, and future identity is "in Christ," and His life, death, and resurrection are in us.

Our Identity in Christ encompasses the foundation of this entire work, which includes the Gospel of Jesus' life, death, and resurrection; the complete order of our salvation; union with Christ; and glorification now and future with Christ. The depths of the Gospel provided for us are far beyond anything we can think or imagine. When we die to our worldly identity, we can experience a new eternal identity. Believing and receiving the life, death, and resurrection of the King allows Jesus's life, death, and resurrection to become part of our identity. As we are "in Christ," we must also remember He is in us, along with the Father and the Holy Spirit (Jn.

14:23). By the power of the Holy Spirit, we become one with the blessed Trinity by being sanctified, conformed, and transformed into His image (Rom. 8:29; 2 Cor. 3:18).

When we understand our Identity in Christ by realizing we are in Christ and Christ is in us, everything is transformed. Ephesians 1:4 teaches that God chose our lives and identity in Christ before the foundation of the world. We must understand our Identity in Christ in the light of knowing that God is not confined to time and space. During Jesus's incarnational life, death, and resurrection, God the Father had already thought of us as being in Christ. That means whatever Christ did during His life, death, and resurrection, it was counted by God as something we did because we were in Christ. God the Father thought of us going through everything Christ went through. If you grasp what I am saying here, it will transform your life.

When Jesus perfectly obeyed the law, the Father thought of us as perfectly obeying the law. When Christ was perfectly about His Father's business, the Father thought of us as being perfectly about our Father's business. When Jesus perfectly prayed, when He shared the Gospel, when He raised the dead, when He healed the blind, when He forgave sins when He taught, when He was raised again from the dead, when He fulfilled the law and prophets, the Father thought of us as being in Christ. If this wasn't taught in the Bible, this would be too amazing for a sinner like me to receive and believe. God's amazing grace is truly amazing good news. His grace still goes much deeper than we can ever imagine.

Because we are in Christ, our sins were also in Christ. Paul tells us in 2 Corinthians 5:21, "God made Him who knew no sin to be sin on our behalf, so that we might become the righteousness of God in Him." In Christ alone, before the foundation of the world, we were forgiven and made righteous. Romans 3:23 says, "that the wages of sin is death," but Jesus was without sin. The love of God is seen in the fact that the Father saw all our sins—past, present, and future—as being in Christ. Christ died and was separated from His Father because Christ took our sins as we were in Christ. Christ died on the cross for our sins, not His. The plot of God's grace just continues to thicken. It was not only our sins that were in Christ but also our lives, past, present, and future were in Christ. Christ paid a very high price for our lives (1 Cor. 6:20). Our lives were completely bought by Christ, allowing us to be in Christ. We have not only been credited with Christ's perfect life and righteousness, but we are also united with Christ's death. Paul says in Romans 6:3, "Or do you not know that all of us who have been baptized into Christ Jesus have been baptized into His death." Paul also says in Galatians 2:20, "I have been crucified with Christ and it is no longer I who live, but Christ lives in me." The Father also saw us as being buried and crucified with Christ (Rom. 6:4-5). I pray you are beginning to see the grace. The Father saw us alive with Christ, buried with Christ, raised up with Christ, blessed with every spiritual blessing in Christ, and seated us with Christ in the heavenly places.

As the Father saw us in Christ when He was on the earth, the Father now sees Christ in us as

What Now?

we are on the earth. The Father sees Christ in everything we do now and in the future. It is no longer about what we do; it is about what Christ has done. Our future is seen in Christ's life, death, and resurrection, living again in us in the present and the future. Paul talks about this incredible mystery of the church in Colossians 1:27: "To whom God willed to make known what is the riches of the glory of this mystery among the Gentiles, which is *Christ in you*, the hope of glory" (emphasis mine). Paul also says in Galatians 2:20, "Christ lives in me." Now that we are no longer a thought in God's mind, we have been given spiritual life to be in an actual relationship with Christ through all the blessings of salvation in the present.

When we understand that our identity rests in the fact that Christ already perfected us and resides within us, it destroys the root of Satan's kingdom pride, lies, and deceptions. Pride is the root of all evil and always goes before the fall. Knowing Christ has made us perfectly righteous compels us to do nothing in this world apart from Christ; trusting in our new identity in Christ, we can do all things through Him who lives within us (Jn. 15:5). We develop incredible humility and dependence as the Holy Spirit gives us incredible confidence, not in self, but in Christ the King working through us (Gal. 2:20; Rom. 15:18; Phil. 4:13). The Holy Spirit conforms us to the life, death, and resurrection of Christ. We participate in the perfect life of Christ that has been credited to us; we die and suffer with Him in death, and we resurrect with Him in power. To become empowered, we enter into our identity in Christ with the authority and power of the King and His kingdom, which means all our actions must be surrendered and obedient to the King "in Christ" and His kingdom. Many Christians will never experience their full God-given identity because of their refusal to be obedient, humble themselves, and surrender. Again, it is the Holy Spirit who produces wisdom of our identity in Christ that, in turn, produces humility and dependence. Our part in the process is twofold: we first simply believe and receive all Christ has done for us through His life, death, and resurrection; second, we humble ourselves and cry out to the Holy Spirit to fill us with more of Christ and less of us. The Holy Spirit will then transform those who are humble and dependent.

The resurrection power, the power-filled identity, can occur at any time during the Christian life when we surrender completely to the King. He unleashes His presence and His kingdom within us. Our new identity will lead to godly wisdom. Wisdom enables Christians to look back on their lives and accomplishments, realizing it was only the work of Christ in us that counts for eternity. Anything we have done through our strength will perish. This provides us with a sense of closure and completeness so that we can accept death without fear because we discovered our identity in Christ, along with an incredible hope of the promises of God that will be awaiting us in heaven.

After just finishing this book, I learned a big lesson. My life motto has always been "All for Jesus." If I am truly All for Jesus, Jesus should be enough in any crisis. The reality was, He wasn't enough. When crises came into my life, I began

What Now?

questioning God. Just like Lucifer, just like Adam and Eve. What do you do when a crisis comes into your life? I looked to the crisis, which causes more crises, and it created a lack of trust in God. I began questioning what God was doing. I entered into an *Identity Crisis*.

The past year has been the most difficult year of my life. Many people would question how God can allow so much hardship? I began to question how God can allow so much suffering? Then I remembered the hardships of Christ. I remembered that through Jesus' suffering, He was perfected (Heb. 2:10-18). Do we really want to be like Christ? God's ways are not our ways, and I remembered the prophet in Isaiah 55:8-9:

> *"For My thoughts are not your thoughts, Nor are your ways My ways," declares the Lord. "For as the heavens are higher than the earth, So are My ways higher than your ways And My thoughts than your thoughts."*

I asked myself, what is the purpose of all this suffering? I began to understand God uses suffering to rid us of our dependence on the things of Satan's world. If you looked at why we suffer, it is all related to our selfish desires for the things of the world. Why am I not healthy? Why don't I have more money? When the things of this world are stripped from us, we suffer the things of this world that will perish to inherit that which will never perish. But this is where the rubber meets the road of our faith. Is Jesus enough? We come down with cancer; is Jesus enough? We lose a child; is Jesus enough? We lose our job; is Jesus enough? We lose everything; is Jesus enough? The Father sent us His most prized possession, His one and only Son. The Father knew before the foundation of the world that Jesus would be enough.

At some point in our lives, we must realize that Jesus is enough. What He offers is infinitely more than anything this world can offer us. Our suffering causes crises in our lives, so we repent of the things of this world and become completely dependent on Jesus. Jesus is enough. Even if we are led to the slaughter like sheep, Jesus is enough. That is why we are told to rejoice in our sufferings, because our sufferings are making us more like Jesus. Remember His suffering. Becoming like Jesus through suffering is one of our many blessings. We must turn from the crisis and turn to Christ. We must not be conformed to the ways of the world but be transformed by the renewing of our minds to understand God's will through suffering (Rom. 12:2).

One of my greatest fears is to not live this power-filled identity that Christ has given to me through His life, death, and resurrection; to stand before God telling Him Jesus wasn't enough; to stand before Jesus in all His glory and power and realize all I could have been in Christ, all I could have done for Him with the power that was my divine inheritance for the taking; saying to Him, "If I only knew then what I know now." We have one chance, one shot, before we stand before Jesus; let's pray that we make that day count. Jesus has so much more for us beyond all we can even begin to think or imagine. I don't claim to have experienced all He has for me, but my theology is not based on my experience; it is based on the words of our sovereign King. I press on toward the upward call of Christ Jesus the King. If the Jesus of the Bible is truly as indescribable as the Bible clearly states, what the heck are we waiting for!

But seek first My kingdom and My righteousness, and all these things will be added to you.
— Jesus

Notes

CHAPTER 1

¹True Discipleship, accessed January 1, 2018, http://williammacdonald.blogspot.com/.
²True Discipleship, accessed January 1, 2018, http://williammacdonald.blogspot.com/.
³ Henry Chadwick, *Saint Augustine Confessions* (Sagamore Beach: Academx Publishing Services, 2005), 3.
⁴The Screwtape Letters accessed January 2, 2018, http://www.simplechurchathome.com/Why.html.

CHAPTER 2

⁵Jack Deere, *Surprised by the Power of the Spirit* (Grand Rapids: Zondervan, 1993), 154.

CHAPTER 7

⁶Wayne Grudem, *Systematic Theology* (Wayne Grudem, 2004), 670.

Bibliography

Deere, Jack. *Surprised by the Power of the Spirit*. Grand Rapids: Zondervan, 1993.

Grudem, Wayne. *Systematic Theology*. Grand Rapids: Zondervan, 2004.

Chadwick, Henry. *True Discipleship*. Sagamore Beach: Academx Publishing Services, 2005.